Scott Witham

Print and Production Finishes for
Promotional_Items

Contents

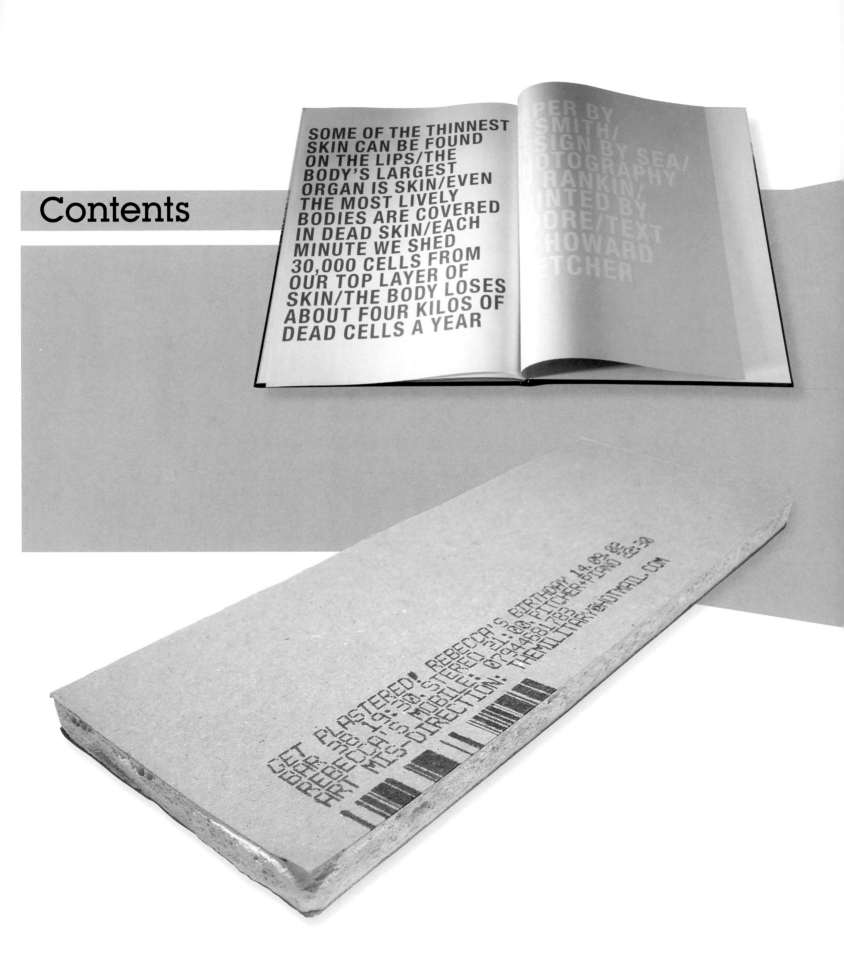

SOME OF THE THINNEST SKIN CAN BE FOUND ON THE LIPS/THE BODY'S LARGEST ORGAN IS SKIN/EVEN THE MOST LIVELY BODIES ARE COVERED IN DEAD SKIN/EACH MINUTE WE SHED 30,000 CELLS FROM OUR TOP LAYER OF SKIN/THE BODY LOSES ABOUT FOUR KILOS OF DEAD CELLS A YEAR

...PER BY
...SMITH/
...SIGN BY SEA/
...OTOGRAPHY
... RANKIN/
...INTED BY
...ORE/TEXT
...SHOWARD
...ETCHER

GET PLASTERED: REBECCA'S BIRTHDAY 14.08.08
GLEEBEC STEREO 21.00 FLTCHER+PIANO 22:30
MEDIA: MOBILE: 07944081783
REBECCA'S DIRECTION:
SPORT MIS-DIRECTION: THEMILITARY@HOTMAIL.COM

Print and Production Finishes for
Promotional_Items

A RotoVision Book

Published and distributed by RotoVision SA
Route Suisse 9
CH-1295 Mies
Switzerland

RotoVision SA
Sales and Editorial Office
Sheridan House, 114 Western Road
Hove BN3 1DD, UK

Tel: +44 (0)1273 72 72 68
Fax: +44 (0)1273 72 72 69
www.rotovision.com

Copyright © RotoVision SA 2007

While every effort has been made to contact owners
of copyright material produced in this book, we
have not always been successful. In the event of
a copyright query, please contact the Publisher.

10 9 8 7 6 5 4 3 2 1

ISBN: 978-2-940361-68-7

Design: Traffic Design Consultants

Reprographics in Singapore by ProVision Pte.

Printed in Singapore by Star Standard Industries (Pte.) Ltd.

Dedicated to my wife Lorna and all
my friends and family

Introduction

Designing for print is easy. That would be true if the world lacked imagination, if designers made no effort, and printers took on only simple four-color work. Thankfully this isn't the world we live in. Designers push at every opportunity, even on limited budgets, manufacturers strive to show off what they can do with the machinery they have, and clients want only the very best to help them stand out from the crowd. This makes the world a far more exciting and testing place when you are a creative designing for print.

Inspirational design is made real through print and production. Good printing and finishing will make a great job even better. Clever use of materials and unusual techniques will ensure that the work gains maximum exposure and praise.

This is every designer's dream—utilizing special finishes, pushing the boundaries of printing, and ensuring that the client keeps coming back for more. It is not an impossible dream. Far from it.

Even on a limited budget there's always room for experimentation. Why spend all the budget on a very expensive paper stock? Find a cheaper one and use what's left to explore other avenues. What happens if you cross-fold, lay down a laminate, and apply a finish on top? Or print onto a metallic then die-cut the sheet? How far will a printer let you go with the funds available?

Every day as designers we should question and experiment, push and develop. It's the only way to keep things really interesting and well away from the mundane. After all, we are living at a time in which the ability and technology to publish outstanding graphic design at a relatively low cost are readily available. This publication celebrates all that is special in print and production for promotional items from around the world. A celebration of bravery, outstanding effort, and simple good luck, it has been a pleasure to compile. You can't always predict the finished effect of the options you choose; you have to try them to find out. Push the boundaries, test the printer, and wow your client. Trust me. They will thank you for it.

Scott_Witham
Traffic_Design_Consultants

The wonderful thing about print, and the reason we use it, is that you can completely encapsulate all the sensorial qualities of a brand. The feel and texture of the paper alone gives the customer an immediate understanding of the depth of the product involved. Great print allows you to then communicate the simple subtleties and nuances of a brand; to surprise and delight. For many designers there's nothing quite like the smell of print.

Jon Lee. Creative Director. 20|20. London

Guest Introductions

At Serial Cut we believe that design should be intelligent, engaging, and memorable. Our aim is always to surpass creative expectations through the use of print finishes or special materials. Our passion for visual sophistication penetrates every stage of the design process, from ideation to development and delivery, and follows through to the very last detail.

Sergio del Puerto. Creative Director
Serial Cut. Madrid

In today's mass-produced, everything-looks-the-same world, the unique and left-field are quite rare. With the myriad special print methods available, one can approximate a number of unique effects through offset litho processes, which is great. But, the old adage holds true: there are no shortcuts in life. Only hand finishing looks like hand finishing. The investment of time and effort cannot be imitated and is thus appreciated for what it is: the signature of the designer as a tangible reflection of the design process itself.

Peter Crnokrak. Creative Director
±. Montréal

At Märang we feel it is very important to involve materials and other production matters early in the creative process, and tie them in to the overall development of the idea. We think of materials as critical to the concept as opposed to simply dressing up an idea. Materials can sometimes even be the starting point in the creative process: extensive ideas can evolve simply from connecting a material with key elements in the initial design brief. An intelligent use of materials will always help communicate emotional values.

Henrik Persson. Creative Director
Märang. Stockholm

A piece of meat is just a piece of meat if there is no proper preparation. A good chef chooses a fine cut, the right heat, selected spices, and the best way to present the dish. This makes the experience 10 times better. A designer's job is the same; to impress, engage, and stimulate the consumer. Smart brands know that they need to invest in proper communication materials if they want to stay in business. A good design can get the job done 100%; a good design with great finishes can get the job done 110%.

Roy Poh. Creative Director. **Kinetic.** Singapore

We live in a world densely populated by design. It surrounds us and we interact with it. Differentiating brands and products from one another has become increasingly difficult. The need for design to stand out has never been so important. We believe in creating an idea, bringing it to life with creativity, and following it right through to the smallest detail. This attention to detail is often most effectively demonstrated through innovation at the production stage. The use of unusual and interesting materials, printing techniques, and finishes provide the icing on the cake, differentiating the ordinary from the extraordinary.

Debora Berardi. Director
Inaria. London

Ever notice how almost every kid who walks along a corrugated wall will run their hand along it as they pass by? As a sidekick to our sense of sight, our sense of touch enhances the visual information that we process. If you can harmonize the two, you'll give your communications a powerful punch. A perfect integration of printing techniques, materials, and design can convey qualitative information both literally and expressively, consciously and subconsciously. The packaging isn't just a vehicle to deliver a message; it's an integral part of the message itself.

Steve Watson. Creative Director
Turnstyle. Seattle

Three seconds is the average attention span an audience will give a message. We want to give them something that needs to be looked at a little longer, a little closer. Something they want to look at. Something they want to keep. Printing methods and materials often provide the basic idea for the design itself, and with this in mind, we explore every element of the printing and manufacturing process.

Challenge yourself, challenge the printer, surprise the viewer, and get noticed!

Pascal Cools. Creative Director
Sound in Motion. Antwerp

Formats

#001
Nike

+**Design Firm** Electrolychee

+**Website** www.electrolychee.com

+**Client** Nike

+**Creative Director** Electrolychee

+**Designer** Electrolychee

+**Printer/Production** Electrolychee

Nike commissioned Electrolychee to render an art piece inspired by its last collection of "Flight" basketball shoes. Electrolychee's concept was based on its own fictional story of how to harness the power of flight. As Electrolychee loves working with illustrations, it made its piece look like a large-scale 3-D illustrated page. It hired a local carpenter to work on the manually printed and acrylic-painted plywood panels that were then cut to shape.

Electrolychee didn't find it difficult to produce because they are highly experienced in handpainting and finishing. If any difficulty was experienced during construction, it was beating the deadline date for transportation and installation of the display.

#002
Land Securities

+**Design Firm** Hat-Trick Design
+**Website** www.hat-trickdesign.co.uk
+**Client** Land Securities

+**Creative Directors** David Kimpton,
 Jim Sutherland, Gareth Howat
+**Printer/Production** Gavin Martin

Land Securities needed a promotional sales brochure for its luxury penthouse The View in Victoria, London. The front cover showed the property's fantastic views over London—a photograph was taken from the penthouse overlooking London and was framed as a limited-edition print.

The brochure is a stunning piece of promotional literature. It is printed on Robert Horne, GF Smith, and Tullis Russell papers (text: 170gsm Parilux Matt; intro sheet: 130gsm Transclear; covers: 350gsm Duplexed Colorplan Pristine White, 1,750 micron Duplex t; endpapers: 250gsm Invercote). The cover text is debossed with a spot clear foil blocking.

Translucent papers

By printing conventional full-color litho onto translucent papers such as 130gsm Transclear, Hat-Trick create a multilayered feel for their brochure, allowing text to shine through from the underlying pages.

#003
Hong Leong

+**Design Firm** Kinetic
+**Website** www.kinetic.com.sg
+**Client** Hong Leong Holdings

+**Creative Director** Roy Poh
+**Designers** Pann Lim, Leng Soh
+**Printer/Production** Colourscan PTE

The Tate is a high-end apartment complex located in the center of Singapore. Kinetic carried the shapes and angles of the building's architecture into the brochure itself. The materials used reflect those found in the building's interior and include special soft-textured paper (milk-touch), metal, and leather. Printing effects include die-cuts, hot foil printing, UV varnish, and blind embossing. Kinetic felt it was important for the reader to have something to touch and feel that would give a very clear idea of the quality to expect from the property. Kinetic used 300gsm Star Dream for the die-cut pages. It has a natural shimmer that mimics metal and the weaving is tough enough to withstand the intricate die-cuts. The design of the die-cut was inspired by the building's structural elements. Roy Poh of Kinetic explains, "The edges near the binding side had to be thicker than usual to keep the pages strong. The intricacy of the design and the weight of the paper had to be considered carefully and we did this by producing several mock-ups prior to proceeding."

Forme cuts

Kinetic have cleverly used several forme cuts to create pages that finish unevenly. The forme, once mounted in the press, will cut and crease the paper rather than printing it in order to create this effect. Any letterpress can be used, cylinder or platen.

#004
Boss Print

+**Design Firm** Hat-Trick Design
+**Website** www.hat-trickdesign.co.uk
+**Client** Boss Print

+**Creative Directors** David Kimpton,
Jim Sutherland, Gareth Howat
+**Printer/Production** Boss Print

Boss wanted a brochure to demonstrate the abilities of its new press. Designed as a proof bag, the limited-edition hand-delivered brochure provides an antidote to the usual excuses made by printers. Small objects are photographed and enlarged to show perfect detail on the oversized pages. Print included four-color process with spot gloss and matte varnishes backed up with a screen-printed cover. The entire job was printed by Boss using satin-screen and vegetable-base inks on McNaughton's 200gsm Hannoart Gloss, 200gsm Hannoart Silk, 200gsm Challenger Offset, and corrugated board.

"the finishers burnt down at the weekend..."

Reduced page size

By printing internal pages that are smaller than the outer cover, Boss Print are able to show off their folding and binding skills using various paper stocks, including cardboard, even at a very large scale.

"the price of paper has gone up again – due to deforestation..."

you're not going to this but...that's all very well but the thing is... is more concerned me, however...I'm really sorry about this, it's just that...you'll never guess what, but in actual fact...nobody could have foreseen this, but it just so happens...this has been totally out of my control and to tell you the truth...

"you'll never match that from cmyk..."

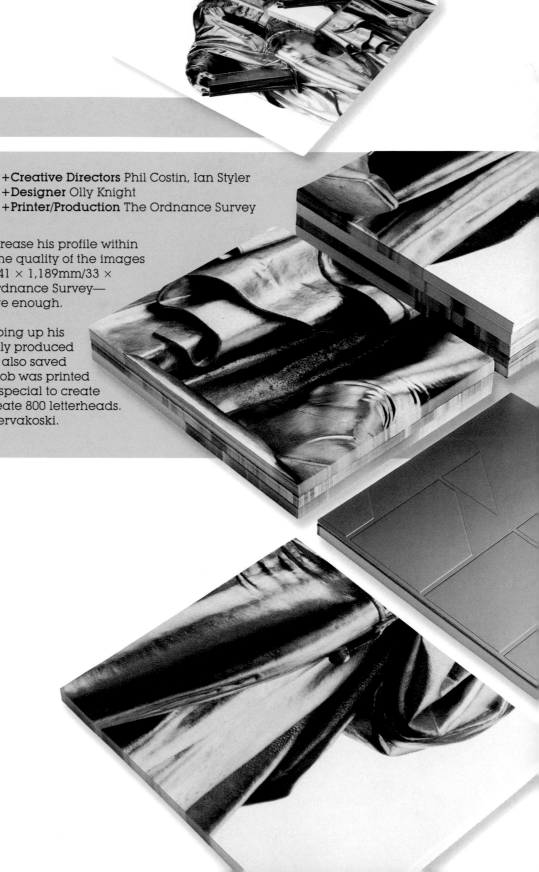

#005
Lee Mawdsly

+**Design Firm** Mode
+**Website** www.mode-online.co.uk
+**Client** Lee Mawdsly

+**Creative Directors** Phil Costin, Ian Styler
+**Designer** Olly Knight
+**Printer/Production** The Ordnance Survey

Lee Mawdsly approached Mode to help increase his profile within the creative industry. Mode's approach let the quality of the images speak for themselves. A series of large A0 (841 × 1,189mm/33 × 46¾in) format posters was printed by The Ordnance Survey—the only company with a printing press large enough.

Lee's stationery range was formed by chopping up his posters at the time of production. This not only produced a very striking and memorable identity, but also saved significantly on production costs. The entire job was printed using 4-color process with a single metallic special to create 800 posters, 50 of which were trimmed to create 800 letterheads. The stock used was 60gsm Tercoat Plus by Tervakoski.

Maximizing print

By printing large-format posters (A0: 841 × 1,189mm/33 × 46¾in) and cutting the excess posters down to A4 (210 × 297mm/8⅛ × 11⅝in), Mode were able to create a range of A4 letterheads that the client could overprint as and when required. A great way to get maximum value from print.

#006
Sensual

+**Design Firm** Sensual
+**Website** www.sensual.pl
+**Client** Sensual

+**Creative Director** Pawel Przybylski
+**Designer** Pawel Przybylski
+**Printer/Production** Sensual

Sensual, a Polish design house, created its own visual identity and promotional material in-house. The base of Sensual's identity and brand image is a square with a main background color of black. Sensual back this up with three intense extra colors to form the complete set of corporate colors. By then taking these core elements outdoors to photograph, Sensual created their portfolio in a unique manner. The shots are displayed in their printed material and online marketing.

#007
Akina

+**Design Firm** Akina
+**Website** www.akina.com.au
+**Client** Akina

+**Creative Director** Lang Leav
+**Photographer** Haline Ly
+**Printer/Production** Lang Leav

The Bear Massacres is a fashion label for Akina's first collection. Akina needed to create a high-impact brochure that would reflect the disturbing gothic nature of the label and its first collection. It was important to Akina to create something that would be seen as slightly odd and yet beautiful. The brochure has successfully helped Akina to capture the attention of buyers in the Australian and Japanese market. Materials used included 120gsm Epson Matt Heavyweight paper, rivets, leathered cord, and various hand-cut embellishments. The brochure was printed on an Epson 129.

Die-cut

Akina have cleverly placed this die-cut to give the work the look and feel of a vintage photo frame. Die-cutting uses sharp metal rules mounted onto blocks for stamping a decorative or unusual shape out of paper or board.

Casebound

<u>Pelé</u> is protected by a solid outer card cover with the inner signatures glued into place. The outer card is covered with colored fabric, allowing it to be embossed or screen printed to give a highly finished, professional look.

#008
Gloria Books

+**Design Firm** Märang
+**Website** www.marang.com
+**Client** Gloria Books Ltd.

+**Creative Director** Mikael Friden
+**Designer** Märang
+**Printer/Production** Various

This limited-, luxury-edition of <u>Pelé</u> was specially commissioned for the promotion and launch of the standard edition of the book. At 450 × 350mm (18 × 14in), and bound in silk, this collectible book weighs 16kg (35⅓lb), contains over 300,000 words, including exclusive new text from Pelé himself, and over 1,700 images. With only 2,500 copies worldwide, <u>Pelé</u> is closer to a limited-edition work of art than a book. It comes in two versions: <u>Carnival Edition</u> (Nos 1–150; $7,000 (c. £4,000)) and <u>Samba Edition</u> (Nos 151–2500; $2,800 (c. £1,600)). All copies are individually signed by Pelé with the <u>Carnival Edition</u> also signed by all surviving members of the World Cup-winning 1970 Brazil team. <u>Pelé</u> is printed on 2,000gsm semimatte LumiSilk art paper. The cover and presentation case are in Setalux fine silk with calfskin embroidered on the cover. <u>Pelé</u> is printed in eight colors using resilient metallic inks, spot colors, and two different varnishes.

'What more could
you possibly want
in your life than to
have a chance to
work with Pelé?'

JIM TRECKER

star trecker

by Ovais Naqvi

Jim Trecker, head of PR at the Cosmos from 1976, discusses Pelé's impact on football in the US.

Concertina folding
These brochures feature concertina folds, with the long, printed pages folded in and out on themselves in a zigzag.

#009
Georgina Goodman

+**Design Firm** Aloof Design
+**Website** www.aloofdesign.com
+**Client** Georgina Goodman

+**Creative Director** Sam Aloof
+**Designers** Andrew Scrase, Chris Barham
+**Printer/Production** Generation Press

Aloof's spring/summer 2005 promotional brochure for designer Georgina Goodman had to be flexible to accommodate an ever-growing collection of shoes, accessories, and colorways. At the same time, the design and branding needed to remain recognizable. In a very competitive, image-sensitive industry, Aloof's design ensured that Georgina Goodman's marketing material confers desirability on the products and instills confidence in the reader.

The brochure was created from GF Smith papers including Zen 300g, and Colorplan 175gsm and 4,000gsm, with printing and finishing including creasing, gluing, folding, foil blocking, and die-cutting. The covers were made from duplexed sheets. Finishing was carried out by hand, which created lead times that were incredibly difficult to estimate.

#010
The Production Kitchen

+**Design Firm** Blok Design
+**Client** The Production Kitchen

+**Creative Director** Vanessa Eckstein
+**Designer** Vanessa Eckstein
+**Printer/Production** Somerset Graphics

The Production Kitchen is dedicated to producing and printing creative projects for the design and advertising industry. For this project, spare graphics and complex linear patterns were combined to express both the nature of the business and the passion the company has for the print production process itself. There is a certain playfulness in the graphics and slanted text that appears and disappears consistently depending on the application. Blok's choice of materials influenced the experimental aspect of print design: they created a flexible brochure in which parts can be interchanged and updated without having to reprint the entire project.

Foil embossing

This piece features a casebound card and fabric cover with foil embossing. In this process, a heated metal block is used to apply foil to, and emboss the cover simultaneously.

#011
Inaria

+**Design Firm** Inaria
+**Website** www.inaria-design.com
+**Client** Inaria

+**Creative Directors** Andrew Thomas, Debora Berardi
+**Designers** Anna Leaver, Anup Sharma-Yun, Anita Cassetta, Andrew Thomas
+**Printer/Production** CTD London

To celebrate its first five years, Inaria, an award-winning brand design consultancy based in London, designed and published a book to showcase the best of its identity, print, and digital media projects. Entitled <u>High Five</u>, the book demonstrates Inaria's approach to combining original ideas with beautifully crafted work to produce pieces that are intelligent, effective, and uplifting.

Paper was supplied by GF Smith, Winters, and Howard Smith and included 148gsm Monadnock Astrolite Smooth and 90gsm On-Offset. The book was casebound with Brillianta Callandse, printed in 4-color plus spot silver, silver foil embossing, and thread sewn with silver head- and tailbands.

#012
XL Recordings

+**Design Firm** Think Tank Media
+**Website** www.thinktankmedia.co.uk
+**Client** XL Recordings

+**Creative Director** Phil Lee
+**Designer** Phil Laslett
+**Printer/Production** Think Tank Media

XL Recordings commissioned London-based Think Tank Media to create
a series of huge-format Christmas Crackers as upmarket branded client gifts.
Five crackers were branded with some of XL's current acts, including The Prodigy,
The White Stripes, and Basement Jaxx. Finishing included silk seal on the
crackers, acetate window affixed to the box made
from single-sided coated 300gsm board with
red ribbon ties. Each cracker contained
a bespoke gift.

#013

±

+**Design Firm** ±
+**Website** www.plusminus.ca
+**Client** ±

+**Creative Director** Peter Crnokrak
+**Designer** Peter Crnokrak
+**Printer/Production** BGM Imaging

Canadian-based typeface designers ± designed and produced the font as well as the packaging for MNTrL. The booklet showcases the stylistic elements of the typeface in comparison to other modular typefaces and also features rejected letterforms that were not incorporated in the final font. The rejected letterforms are hand-drawn using a light gray Pantone Tria marker and then crossed out in red marker. Additionally, all of the typeface data and design credits are filled in by hand using a Sharpie black marker. The hand application is used to reflect the manner in which the letterforms were originally created (sheet after sheet of hand-filled 5 × 7 empty grids) and also to symbolize the hand of authorship. Perforation lines were used to create decorative cover elements that mimic the basic letterform reference points (baseline, cap height, letterform width, and x-height). Hand-drawn details were then added—typeface technical and copyright information, etc. Each package is therefore unique.

Gloss-coated stock

Gloss-coated stock has a hard, but smooth surface with a gloss finish. Gloss-coated stock is quicker-drying than uncoated stock, and, as ink does not soak into the paper, it is excellent for reproducing halftone images.

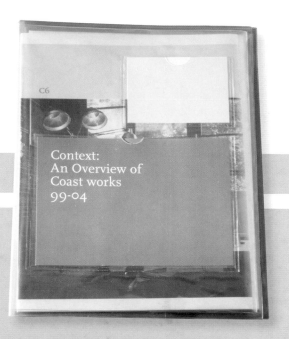

014
Coast Design

+**Design Firm** Coast Design
+**Website** www.coastdesign.be
+**Client** Coast Design

+**Creative Directors** Frederic
 Vanhorenbeke, Ingrid Arquin
+**Printer/Production** Derume Printing

Brussels-based Coast Design wanted to create a special brochure
to celebrate its portfolio of work covering its first five years in business.
The brochure is divided into two sections: work in context and classified.
In the work in context section, Coast wanted to show that graphic design
is a commercial business. For the classified section, Coast wanted to make
a statement of "overflowing" work.

Coast spent a lot of time producing its own photography. It shot many of the
pieces in unusual settings, including a castle interior, parking lot, and forest.

#015
Teague

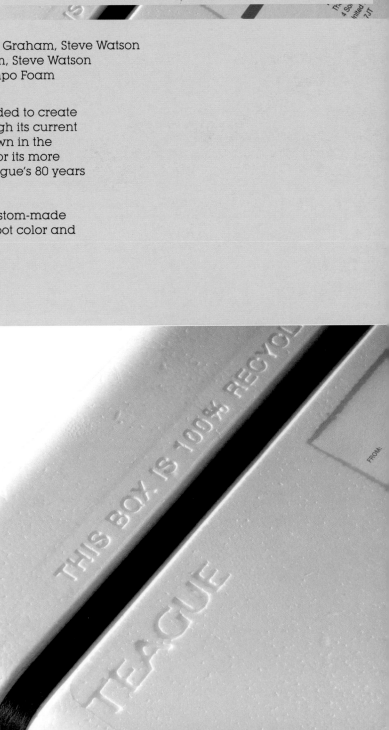

+**Design Firm** Turnstyle
+**Website** www.turnstylestudio.com
+**Client** Teague

+**Creative Directors** Ben Graham, Steve Watson
+**Designers** Ben Graham, Steve Watson
+**Printer/Production** Tempo Foam

The limited-edition (totalling 325) Teague portfolio mailer was intended to create awareness for Teague's unique design perspective as evident through its current body of work. Teague has been around for 80 years and is well known in the industrial design sector as a legacy company, but less well known for its more recent innovative work. The mailer aimed to communicate how Teague's 80 years of experience help to inform its work today.

This bespoke mailer was created with Domtar Luna Matte and a custom-made polystyrene box. It used conventional CMYK printing with a single spot color and was finished with an overall aqueous coating.

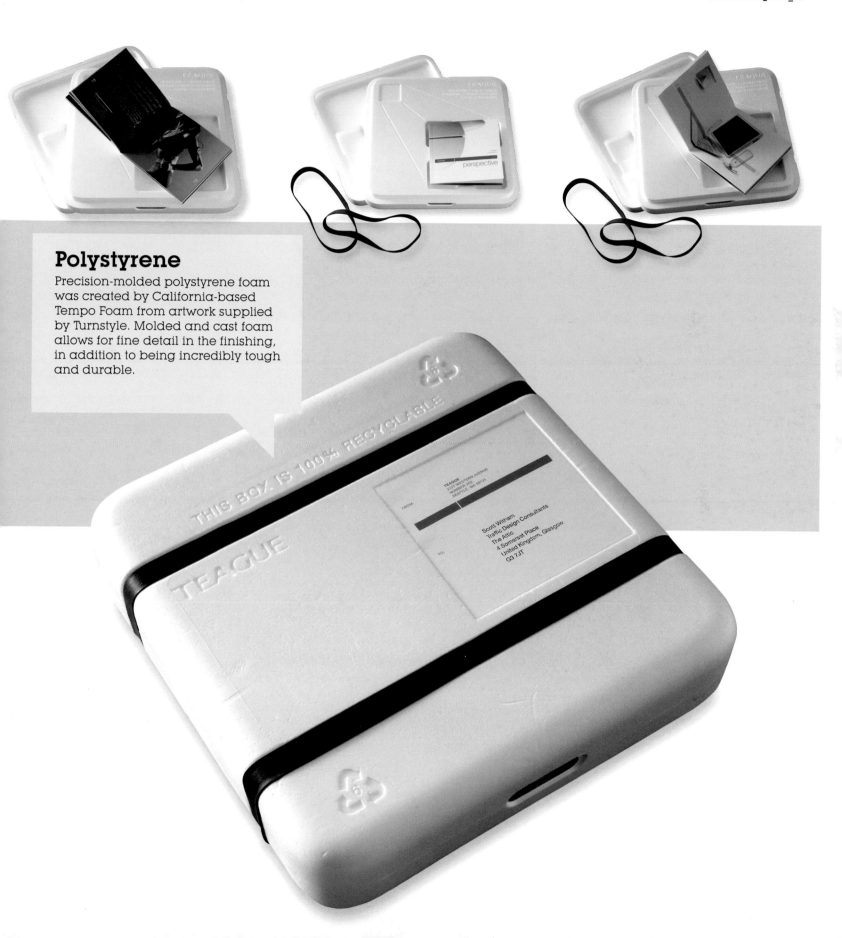

Polystyrene

Precision-molded polystyrene foam was created by California-based Tempo Foam from artwork supplied by Turnstyle. Molded and cast foam allows for fine detail in the finishing, in addition to being incredibly tough and durable.

#016
GF Smith

+**Design Firm** Sea
+**Web** www.seadesign.co.uk
+**Client** GF Smith

+**Creative Director** Bryan Edmonson
+**Designer** Ryan Jones
+**Printer/Production** Moore

Sea was commissioned by paper manufacturer GF Smith to produce a promotional book for the launch of PhoeniXmotion Paper. Sea followed the theme of the human body throughout and merged photography with typography to produce <u>Surface Seduction</u>.

As GF Smith were supplying the paper, this book was able to utilize many weights of PhoeniXmotion Xenon and Xantor papers, including 115, 135, 150, 170, and 250gsm. It was finished with red gloss foil, a stochastic and a conventional screen, with an overall gloss UV and Rhodamine Red touch plate.

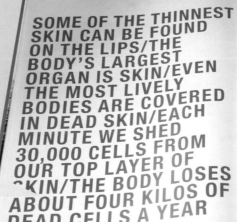

Gloss foil

This process uses extremely thin, colored metal foils that are transferred using a heated printing plate. Available in many colors, and with both gloss and matte finishes, this foil can be printed onto almost any surface or material.

#017
Topshop

+**Design Firm** Design N/A
+**Web** www.design-na.co.uk
+**Client** Topshop

+**Creative Directors** Neil Emery, Adam Thorpe
+**Designer** Design N/A
+**Printer/Production** Grey & Mcdonald, Artomatic, Glennleigh Print

M250 is a membership card that takes the form of a mirror. It is sent out by clothing retailers Topshop to 250 leading fashion editors, stylists, and celebrities, entitling them to a personalized shopping service. Each year the style of mirror is changed. To date it has ranged from antique to smoked to bronze. It is cut, beveled, and polished from 6mm (c. ¼in) glass. This year the square gray mirror was screen printed on both sides, then vacuum sealed within a large square polythene bag, also screen printed, with 250 dots. The bag was then packed in a white leather, hole-punched pouch, in a cube-shaped, gloss white box. Each box was addressed by hand with luminous rub-down lettering.

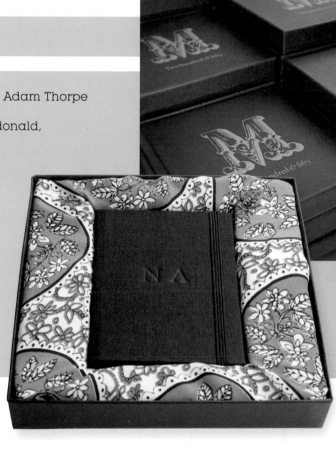

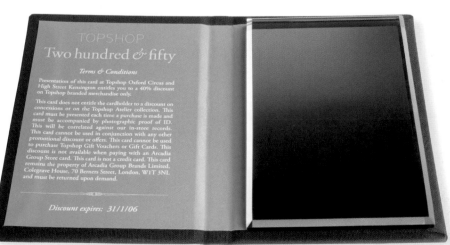

Materials

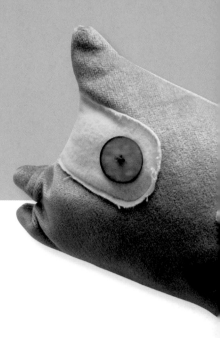

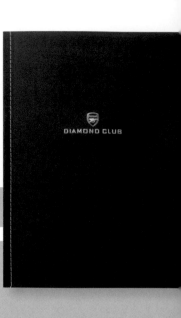

#018
Arsenal Football Club

+**Design Firm** 20|20
+**Website** www.20.20.co.uk
+**Client** Arsenal Football Club

+**Creative Director** Jon Lee
+**Designer** Phillip Mottram
+**Printer/Production** Mathew Brown, Print Solutions

20|20 were recently commissioned to create the exclusive Diamond Club members' lounge and restaurant for the new Arsenal Emirates Football Stadium. The Diamond Club is destined to be the most exclusive place in the world to watch football and has already attracted membership from international royalty and a host of A-list celebrities. "The brochure is designed to emulate the look and feel of the Diamond Club environment and to replicate Arsenal's legendary stories through embossing, blind embossing, and foil blocking," states Jon Lee of 20|20. "The only difficulty was with allowing the gold ink enough time to dry so we could then emboss the graphics." Stocks used throughout included 140gsm Splendergel and 200gsm Nettuno Carrubo, both by Fedrigoni.

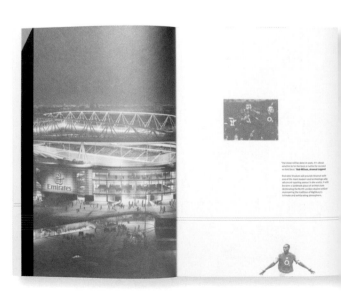

30s CHAMPIONS

Diamond Club takes its inspiration from the 1930s the pivotal decade in the history of Arsenal Football Club.

Herbert Chapman guided the Club to their first ever trophy – The FA Cup – in 1930, and by the time the Second World War broke out, the Gunners had added four league titles, and two more FA Cups. The success was achieved through flowing, inventive, counter-attacking football. In short, the Thirties was a glorious era which was to define the future of Arsenal.

It is befitting that Diamond Club seeks to capture the ambience of such a glorious decade.

Spot metallic inks

All standard litho printing creates colors from different combinations of cyan, magenta, yellow, and black. Spot colors and spot metallics are special inks not generated by this 4-color process, but purchased or matched to specific color systems, such as the PANTONE® system.

Showthrough

By printing onto a very lightweight paper stock, Turnbull Grey made use of the showthrough from one side of the printed page to the other. This was highlighted by placing the posters in special display lightboxes.

#019

Turnbull Grey

+**Design Firm** Turnbull Grey
+**Website** www.turnbullgrey.co.uk
+**Client** Turnbull Grey

+**Creative Director** Chris Turnbull
+**Designer** Chris Turnbull
+**Printer/Production** Waltham Litho

Double Sided was a self-initiated exhibition of Turnbull Grey's personal and commercial work. The poster/invitation reflected this by being printed double-sided on lightweight paper to show how the two sides interact to become a complete package. They were displayed in lightboxes in the entrance to the show. The invitations were produced on Fenner Paper's ultralight 60gsm Offenbach, printed in three special colors, and folded twice. The main problem experienced by Turnbull Grey was finding a printer who would print large areas of color onto the very thin paper stock. Such a lightweight material can start to fall apart when large areas of ink are printed onto it, damaging rollers and blankets on the press. Turnbull Grey also wanted to print on both sides of the material. The A3 (297 × 420mm/11¾ × 16½in) poster had to be printed in the middle of a B2 (707 × 500mm/27¾ × 19¾in) sheet and trimmed to avoid this. Waltham Litho offered to help to get the project going—with its patience and help, the poster/invitation was produced to a very high standard.

#020
Claretduskymoonpie

+**Design Firm** Claretduskymoonpie
+**Website** www.claretduskymoonpie.com
+**Client** Claretduskymoonpie

+**Creative Director** Haline Ly
+**Designer** Haline Ly
+**Printer/Production** Haline Ly

The Claretduskymoonpie toys were made to send out to art directors to promote Haline Ly as an illustrator. Each toy is unique and handmade using fabric, felt, buttons, magnets, squeakers, and polyester filling.

#021
The Ritz Club

+**Design Firm** Deep
+**Website** www.deep.co.uk
+**Client** The Ritz Club

+**Creative Director** Grant Bowden
+**Designer** Lory Serra
+**Printer/Production** Fernedge

Deep created this remarkable brochure to market all the Ritz brands—the hotel, the club, fine jewelry, and online gaming. Materials used included 300gsm Curious Touch Soft Milk and 250gsm Fedrigoni. The brochure was perfect bound, printed in seven colors, and featured a silver foil block.

During production Deep's biggest problem was the marking of the cover material, Curious Touch Soft Milk, which picked up dirt very easily, especially due to its soft feel. To ensure the brochures reached the client in perfect condition, each brochure had to be protected with tissue paper when packed. The cover material caused much interest and comment on its unusual feel—unfortunately it also seems to mark very easily and quickly.

Perfect binding

In this method of binding, signatures are glued to the cover and then brought together with strips of adhesive. While not as strong as conventional stitching, this allows for greater flexibility of pages, and for different stocks to be compiled in various sequences.

RITZ CLUB
LONDON
Mr Andrew M. Love
Chief Executive of The Ritz Club
is delighted to invite you to attend
A Champagne Reception
on

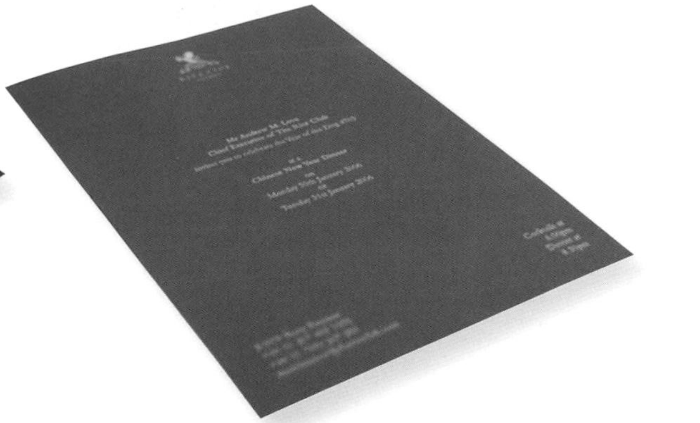
Mr Andrew M. Love
Chief Executive of The Ritz Club

THE RITZ CLUB
RITZ CLUB
LONDON

THE RITZ CLUB
RITZ CLUB
LONDON
ou are visiting the hotel for the first time
urn visit, on behalf of Stephen Boxall,
anager and myself, I welcome you to
ondon.
are a resident at the hotel, may I
o enjoy complimentary membership
Club. Open from 12noon until 6am,
ovides a luxurious and sophisticated
reflecting the facilities that you
Ritz Hotel.
RITZ CLUB
LONDON

#022

Pablo Gallery

+**Design Firm** Inksurge
+**Website** www.inksurge.com
+**Client** Pablo Gallery

+**Creative Directors** Rex Advincula, Joyce Tai
+**Designers** Rex Advincula, Joyce Tai
+**Printer/Production** Pablo Gallery

Inksurge is a collective design studio (based in Manila, Philippines) that enjoys working on any form of experimental design. It was therefore a perfect brief for Inksurge when it was asked to brand and create work for Pabhaus, a graphic design/furniture show featuring Manila's graphic design talents.

For the lamp, Inksurge challenged the supplier to print its design inside out so that, when the lamp is switched off, you can't see the design. The materials used included ceramic tiles, Narra wood, and canvas with digital printing and laser etching.

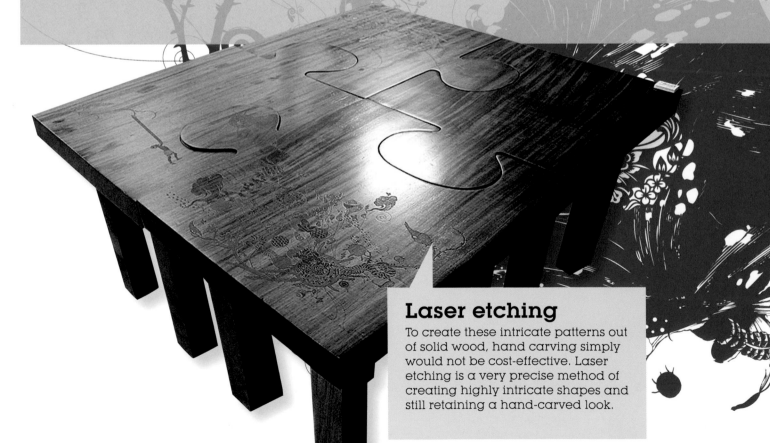

Laser etching
To create these intricate patterns out of solid wood, hand carving simply would not be cost-effective. Laser etching is a very precise method of creating highly intricate shapes and still retaining a hand-carved look.

#023
PT Paperina Dwijaya

+**Design Firm** Jejak
+**Website** www.jejak.net
+**Client** PT Paperina Dwijaya

+**Creative Director** Jacky Halim
+**Designer** Jejak Team
+**Printer/Production** Harapan Prima

Jejak designed the Watudu Card—a gift from Indonesian paper manufacturer PT Paperina Dwijaya to visitors to its stand at the Forum Grafika Digital Indonesia. The challenge was to create an interesting gift that could create a buzz in the graphic design world and display the client's various products. The Watudu Card is a game to play when at a loss for things to do on weekends, and consists of 52 cards, each with a different idea/activity.

All paper stocks used were from PT Paperina Dwijaya with specialist print finishing including hot metal, embossing, debossing, perforation, gloss/matte varnish, die-cutting, etc. The public's response during the FGDI was explosive. Within four days 10,000 sets of Watudu Card were produced and distributed. This project was used widely by graphic design students and industry practitioners as paper and printing technique reference cards.

#024
FLOCKS

+**Design Firm** Joliat
+**Website** www.joliat.net
+**Client** FLOCKS

+**Creative Directors** Julie Joliat,
  Christien Meindertsma
+**Designer** Julie Joliat
+**Printer/Production** Repro's, Amsterdam

Joliat created a corporate identity for the Swiss fashion brand FLOCKS. Each garment in the collection was produced from the wool of just one sheep, continuing until the wool was finished. A little passport of the sheep is attached to each jumper. Julia Joliat recalls, "Finding a flock of sheep wasn't as easy as it sounds; creating decent photography of sheep was even more difficult!" Materials used included 120gsm/200gsm Greentop creme and white fabris for the passport cover, which also used a silver foil for the title.

Uncoated stock

Uncoated stock has a rougher surface than coated stock. This quality allows it to absorb more ink, resulting in a duller, but pleasant look and feel. Uncoated paper is simply stock that has not been coated with china clay.

FLOCKS

Christien Meindertsma
Designer
Marconistraat 52
Haven 357
3029 AK Rotterdam
The Netherlands

+31 626 540 843
christien@theseflocks.com
www.theseflocks.com

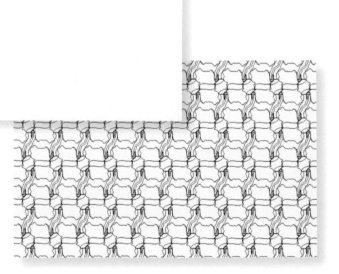

dry clean or hand wash in cool water with a mild soap,
rinse with cool water and squeeze out the water – don't wring,
roll the garment in a towel to remove the excess water,
shape the garment and lay flat to dry.

FLOCKS
PASSPORT

sheep collection fall/winter 2005

FLOCKS PASSPORT	TAG NUMBER B87 012	GARMENT NUMBER SHEEP001
	BREED MERINO/SHETLAND	
	NAME	
	DATE OF BIRTH 04.02.2000	
	SEX FEMALE	
	SIRE TAG NUMBER 7031	DATE OF ISSUE 13 10 2005
	PLACE OF BIRTH SHROPSHIRE	DELIVERED BY FLOCKS, THE NETHERLANDS
	WEIGHT 88.5 KG	

MERINO<SHETLAND<<<<B87012<<<<<<<<<<<<<<<<<<<<<<<
SHEEP001<<<<<<<<<<<<<<<<<<<<<<<<<<<<<<<<<<<<<<<<0

#025
DJPA Partnership

+**Design Firm** Märang
+**Website** www.marang.com
+**Client** DJPA Partnership

+**Creative Director** Henrik Persson
+**Designer** Märang
+**Printer/Production** Märang

Märang designed a Do-It-Yourself themed campaign for a design competition where the organizer, Dutch ad agency DJPA, aimed to headhunt outstanding creatives as well as promoting its own business by using the company color orange. Märang created a Website and promotion kit to advertise the competition. The kit was sent out to leading design schools, as well as the media, in the UK. The CD/media kit packaging was made from thick cardboard found at a dump, a rubber band, and a painting brush dipped in orange paint. Director Henrik Persson recalls, "As the competition theme was 'Do-It-Yourself,' aiming to inspire people to go out to their messy garages looking for inspiration among rusty screws and paint buckets, etc, we wanted to do something with a homemade feel for the promotion kit."

#026
Tate Galleries

+**Design Firm** NB: Studio
+**Website** www.nbstudio.co.uk
+**Client** Tate Galleries

+**Creative Directors** Alan Dye,
  Nick Finney, Ben Scott
+**Designer** Sarah Fullerton
+**Printer/Production** Push

NB: Studio designed a membership pack for the Tate Galleries that provides "added value" to being a member. It set out to create a desirable, must-have product. By creating a distinct style, solely for membership, it generated an exclusive feel extending across a range of items. The studio also wanted to avoid a corporate look, so it shunned the existing Tate color palette in favor of photography of real people interacting with art in any of the four galleries. Working with photographer Matt Stuart, NB: Studio softened the images to make them "Tate." Materials used included 135gsm Gray Colorplan and 150gsm Ikono gloss, with print and finishing including screen-printed white with lithographed black plus four-color litho and UV gloss varnish with a perforated bookmark on the last page.

UV gloss varnish

The pages containing photography were coated with a UV varnish. This liquid varnish, which is heat-dried using ultraviolet light, results in a very hard, glossy, and durable finish.

#027

Cinéma du Parc

+**Design Firm** ±
+**Web** www.plusminus.ca
+**Client** Cinéma du Parc

+**Creative Director** Peter Crnokrak
+**Designer** Peter Crnokrak
+**Printer/Production** Jones & Morris

This three-part series of promotional posters showcases Cinéma du Parc's special screening of politically charged auteur films from the 1960s (including Fahrenheit 451 and If....). The second part features François Truffault's Masculin, féminin, the poster for which features a key quote from the film set against a bubblegum camouflage pattern and a meta-narrative image of a teddy bear sporting a gas mask. An all-stencil type set and hand-appliquéd elements have been used to represent political resistance. Additionally, the hand-drawn elements provide a noticeable contrast to the vector-drawn graphics when the posters are lit from behind. They create an aesthetic that cannot be duplicated with a single-step process.

Lambda plastic

Lambda printing is the latest in state-of-the-art digital technology for producing high-quality photographic outputs from disc. Lambda prints are produced by transferring images directly from computer-generated digital files to reflective or backlit photographic materials without the need for a negative. The material is then processed in the same manner as traditional photography, by developing it in a "wet" film processor.

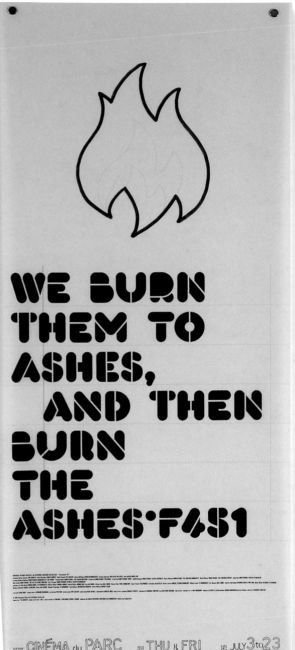

TRAVIS : DEATH TO THE OPPRESSOR,

JOHNNY: THE

RESISTANCE,

WALLACE : LIBERTY,

TRAVIS: ONE MAN

CAN CHANGE THE

WORLD

WITH A BULLET

IN THE

RIGHT PLACE

...REAL BULLETS.

if....

WE BURN
THEM TO
ASHES,
AND THEN
BURN
THE
ASHES·F451

Cinéma PARC mon.-Fri. may 1 to 7
514 281 1900 3575 du Parc 5:30 and 8:30

CINÉMA du PARC THU & FRI JULY 3 to 23
514 281 1900 3575 ave. du PARC 7:00 and 8:00

#028
W. Het Oosten

+**Design Firm** QuA Associates
+**Website** www.qua.nl
+**Client** W. Het Oosten

+**Creative Director** Erik Schuur
+**Designer** Erik Schuur
+**Printer/Production** Oscar Flier

Het Oosten is one of the leading real-estate companies in Amsterdam. One of its important contributions is the realization of a housing project close to the Bos en Lommerplein.

QuA's concept paid special attention to the public image that Bos en Lommer currently has. Bos en Lommer is a neighborhood with relatively numerous social problems. However, it also has the youngest population and a large number of entrepreneurs and start-up companies. Confronting these local issues, the atmosphere found on the streets inspired QuA's design work. In this way, QuA developed a positive and challenging look and feel that communicates the neighborhood's character in an honest way. Connections were made between a very colorful, clean Dutch atmosphere and the more exotic street culture of Bos en Lommer.

Polypropylene

Polypropylene is a flexible plastic that can be used for covers in place of standard card. It is available in many vibrant colors and with many different textured finishes, from a canvas effect to a hammer finish.

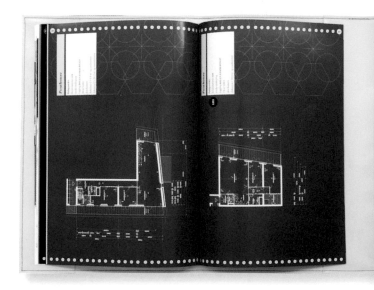

#029
The North Face

+**Design Firm** Saturday
+**Website** www.saturday-london.com
+**Clients** GAS, The North Face

+**Creative Director**
 Erik Tarsknsson
+**Designer** Saturday
+**Printer/Production** Saturday

Saturday was commissioned by GAS and The North Face to design a
limited-edition CD compilation. Two versions were made: one in solid
wood with engraved graphics and the other, more traditional, in paper.
The CD was sold exclusively in North Face stores.

#030
SAP

+**Design Firm** Sixfive Design
+**Website** www.sixfive.com
+**Clients** SAP, The Works London

+**Creative Director** Al Kennedy
+**Designer** Sixfive Design
+**Printer/Production** Various

The Monaco Grand Prix in Monte Carlo is one of the most prestigious events in the sports calendar. SAP, corporate partner of Team McLaren Mercedes F1, host a white-glove hospitality program at the event. Guests of SAP received a distinctive metal invitation with laser-etched detail, along with a handmade book that previewed the race weekend and outlined its history. The metal invitations (0.5mm steel) were die-cut, laser etched, and placed in wallet featuring black foil blocking and debossed text on 540gsm Ebony Colorplan from GF Smith. The casebound book also features black foil blocking and debossing. Text pages were printed in 4-color with silver foil blocking on GF Smith's Citrine Colorplan, and finished with silver gilding.

Gilded edge

The designers chose to finish the book with silver gilding applied once the edges were trimmed. This replicated and continued the theme of the silver-foil blocking on the cover and spine.

SAP chooses its Partners carefully. However sometimes this choice is actually quite simple. Any time you have the opportunity to join an industry leader, you can't pass it up.

Since McLaren's formation in 1966 they have become one of the most successful teams in Formula One, winning 11 drivers championships and 8 constructors championships. That's why it was easy for SAP to select Team McLaren Mercedes as a Partner.

As a guest of SAP you will have exclusive access to the world's greatest racing team at the world's greatest motor race.

Welcome to Team McLaren Mercedes at the Monaco Grand Prix.

#031
Spook

+**Design Firm** Standard13
+**Website** www. standard13.com
+**Client** Spook

+**Creative Director** Wendy Cooper
+**Designer** Wendy Cooper
+**Printer/Production** Brand Print

Spook is an independent Melbourne fashion label. These promotional materials were produced to launch its brand and inaugural collection in fall 2003. The general invitation was printed onto a swing tag presented alongside a catalog (both machine stitched). The catalog was hung on a miniature coat hanger that could fold out into a 396 × 228mm (15¾ × 9in) poster. It was designed so that as each section was unfolded, it revealed a new item from the collection, showing the contact details last. VIP guests received their invitation on a machine-stitched cotton scarf. Materials used included cotton, 300gsm and 170gsm Munken Lynx White, and fuse wire. The sewing machine used by Standard13 had no inbuilt memory, so all the sewing had to be done in one session.

#032
Almap BBDO

+**Design Firm** Superbacana Design
+**Website** www.superbacanadesign.com.br
+**Client** Almap BBDO

+**Creative Director** Vivian de Cerqueira Leite
+**Designers** Fernando Dranger, Circe Bernandes
+**Printer/Production** Grafica Copibrasa, Patricia Isler

The advertising agency Almap BBDO commissioned
Superbacana Design to make its relationship
marketing item for International Women's Day.
The gift consists of a small paper box with four small
pure silk pouches with silk screen print, suitable for
organizing those loose objects always found in a
woman's purse. Materials used included 250gsm Duo
Design paper and 200gsm Translucents Orange with
printing in 4-color offset.

Silk-screen printing
Silk-screen printing is a traditional
form of printing by which ink is forced
through a stencil glued to a taut
screen. This is a particularly good
method for printing onto fabrics,
boards, or anything that is not able
to be fed through a conventional
printing press.

#033
The YMCA

+**Design Firm** The Apartment
+**Website** www.theapt.com
+**Client** The YMCA

+**Creative Director** Stefan Boublil
+**Designer** Tiziana Haug
+**Printer/Production** Corporate Communications

The first YMCA basketball court in New York was recently converted into a luxurious loft and this invite was designed to celebrate the completion of the construction. The invite unfolds into four panels, each one standing for one season of development. Once the panels are folded and "things" fall into place (end of construction), the actual message can be read.

The invites were printed on Neenah Paper UV Ultra II 17# white, which needed to be dried a day longer than usual before scoring and folding to avoid smearing. Registration had to be perfect for the design to match up correctly. Front and back were printed to achieve a stronger see-through effect.

#034
Rebecca Flounders

+**Design Firm** The Military
+**Website** www.themilitary.co.uk
+**Client** Rebecca Flounders

+**Creative Director** Anthony Antoniou
+**Designer** Anthony Antoniou
+**Printer/Production** Anthony Antoniou

With a production run of just 90, these hand-finished invitations consisted of cut plasterboard sections with stamped artwork. They were created using 9mm (c. ⅜in) British Gypsum Handi-board and a simple rubber die and pad.

Once The Military had decided on the plasterboard format, it wanted to emulate precisely the dot matrix copy on the back of the gypsum sheets for the information on the front. The copy looked as though it had been applied to the sheets in a very quick motion in the factory and had a slight lean to it.

Rubber die

For small print runs, this is a reasonably cheap, effective, and fun way of printing onto awkward or unusual materials. A rubber die with the text cast onto its surface is inked up and stamped onto the material to create handpressed printing.

#035
Joanna Stevenson

+**Design Firm** The Military
+**Website** www.themilitary.co.uk
+**Client** Joanna Stevenson

+**Creative Director** Anthony Antoniou
+**Designer** Anthony Antoniou
+**Printer/Production** Anthony Antoniou

This hand-finished promotional invite was made using cherry lips candy encased in overprinted tracing paper. With a print run of just 120, the tracing paper sheets were fed through a standard photocopier and then hand-scored, folded, and assembled.

Antoniou states, "Managing to get the bag of cherry lips from Woolworths without eating the lot proved to be an exercise in itself. I think I had to make two or three repeat visits by the end of the project—I was operating on a sugar high over the three days that it took to create these pieces."

#036
ShuffleArt

+**Design Firm** Yucca Studio
+**Website** www.yuccastudio.com
+**Client** ShuffleArt

+**Creative Directors** Gerard, Agnes
+**Designers** Gerard, Agnes
+**Printer/Production** Intrapress Pte Ltd.

The idea behind ShuffleArt was to take the clean and simple looks of an iPod and add interest through graphics printed onto a self-adhesive vinyl sticker. The main difficulties encountered were sourcing the right material to apply to the iPod, and finding the right printer to work with this material. With these problems solved and the skins successfully in production, ShuffleArt invited guest designers to create a new range of designs to work alongside their own skins. These were made from self-adhesive vinyl and were screen printed by Intrapress Pte Ltd.

#037
Zoveck Estudio

+**Design Firm** Zoveck Estudio
+**Website** www.zoveck.com
+**Client** Zoveck Estudio

+**Creative Directors** Julio Carrasco, Sonia Romero
+**Designers** Julio Carrasco, Sonia Romero
+**Printer/Production** 75 grados, Alegandro Garcia, Lucy

This doll promotes the creative services of Zoveck Estudio. Based on the popular sports entertainment of wrestling, it represents a Mexican-style hero. It is given as a gift to potential customers and friends and also sold in specialty stores. Zopilote Ramirez is a 100 percent Mexican hero who fights evil, corruption, lazy providers, late-paying customers, annoying mothers-in-law, and stubborn salesmen. He has no special powers or extraordinary strength, nor is he particularly brave. All he has is his mask, cape, and underpants, but he does what he can, whatever way he can, when he can, and if God wills it so. He is created from colored resins and all his clothes are handmade. The packaging is printed in silk screen, three inks on fine cardboard with the inner card offset in 4-color plus one spot.

Injection molding

Injection molding is used to produce quantities of identical plastic items. One of the most common thermo-plastics used for this is high-impact polystyrene (HIPS).

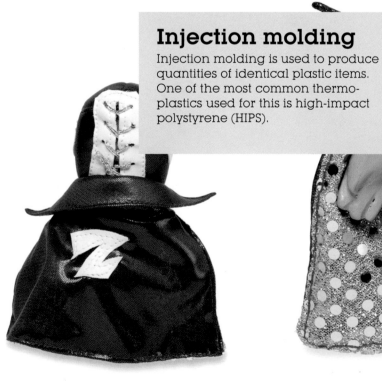

#038
Think Tank Media

+**Design Firms** Airside, Think Tank Media
+**Web** www.airside.co.uk
+**Client** Think Tank Media

+**Creative Director** Airside
+**Designer** Henki Leung
+**Printer/Production** Think Tank Media

Think Tank wanted to produce a marketing tool that reflected not only their creative input, but also the diversity in the work they produce. The result was the Tony Toad book and game. Based on the kids "Misfit" game, the game demonstrates an array of substrates used by Think Tank. The book demonstrates various printing and finishing techniques. Materials used included brown cloth cover, silk, gloss on 200gsm uncoated and Challenger offset 170gsm. Finishing included debossing onto the cloth front and back cover of the book to semiburn material for greater definition, and sewing the book to allow different finishes, including foiling, embossing, debossing, MFX printing, and metallic inks.

#039
Design People Studio

+**Design Firm** Design People Studio
+**Website** www.designpeople.net
+**Client** Design People Studio

+**Creative Directors** Maria Monferrer, Alehandro Canada
+**Designers** Maria Monferrer, Alehandro Canada
+**Printer/Production** Design People Studio

This promotional pack was created for the launch of Design People Studio. It included introductory text and a log-in form to view a portfolio not available to the general public.

The poster was printed with an allover Pantone color with tints of a further three different Pantone colors laid down. Packs also included business cards, pins, and T-shirts.

#040
Design People Studio

+**Design Firm** Famous Visual Services
+**Website** www.famousclothing.com.au
+**Client** Design People Studio

+**Creative Director** Famous Visual Services
+**Designer** Famous Visual Services
+**Printer/Production** Famous Visual Services

This self-initiated project was initially intended as a self-promotional piece, but has grown into a clothing label. The studio selects a location and then visits it to gather inspiration from the community to create a new range of T-shirts. Once the T-shirts are made, the studio returns to the location to seek out residents who are willing to participate in a photo shoot to promote the range. The best shots are then used in the catalog that displays the range and explains the story behind the project. Items produced include T-shirts, screen-printed pizza boxes, and six pages folded to an A6 (105 × 148mm/4 × 5¾in) pamphlet.

Cross-folding

Cross-folding allows for large-format print to be folded to a more manageable size. Careful consideration must be given to the weight of paper: if it is too heavy it won't fold or lie flat; if it is too light it will foul on folding machines, creating a huge amount of waste. For these posters 170gsm was used.

The
Famous
Fifty

#041
Chiltern St. Studio

+**Design Firm** Iwantdesign
+**Website** www.iwantdesign.co.uk
+**Client** Chiltern St. Studio

+**Creative Directors** John Gilsenan, Bruce Allaway
+**Designer** Iwantdesign
+**Printer/Production** Generation Press

After designing the Chiltern St. Studio branding, Iwantdesign was asked to create two invitations. It used the season's colors (white and gold) in its designs: the men's invitation was on fine bible paper with gold metallic ink and the women's invitation used an opaque white ink silk screened on gold-metal-coated tissue. The only difficulty encountered by Iwantdesign was sourcing the metallic tissue. However, Generation Press found a suitable material and produced the finished product on an almost unprintable 28gsm, metal-coated tissue paper, printing a gold single-sided and a white opaque ink silk screened. The final folding was all done by hand.

Hand-finishing

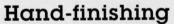

Sometimes hand-finishing is the only way to complete a project. On this occasion the material used was so light, at 28gsm, that it would simply tear and jam in the printer's folding machine. There was no option but to hand-fold each individual invite.

#042
Sound Transmitter

+**Design Firm** Iwantdesign
+**Website** www.iwantdesign.co.uk
+**Client** Sound Transmitter

+**Creative Directors** John Gilsenan, Bruce Allaway
+**Designers** John Gilsenan, Bruce Allaway
+**Printer/Production** Pioneer Print

Iwantdesign created two tour flyers, which were A3 (297 × 420mm/11¾ × 16½in) folded down to A5 (148 × 210mm/5¾ × 8¼in), to promote Sound Transmitter, contemporary music artists from Scandinavia. It chose to use newsprint (45gsm newsprint from Robert Horne Group) as it felt that its fragile quality would offset the powerful nature of the illustrations. John Gilsenan recalls, "Pioneer Print was a great help. Newsprint is tricky to print as it is so fine and can break up. We tried not to saturate the page with too much color and to keep it simple—hence each run was single color. It then had to run the press very slowly, and the same again with the folding machine.

"The project was a quick turnaround with a low budget—we worked on one idea each and chose the newsprint because it is a cheap way to achieve something that looks and feels quality."

Single spot color

Printing in a single spot color matched to a color swatch can yield simple, but striking results, as these posters clearly show. Brighter, bolder colors can be achieved using ready-mixed spot colors rather than 4-color process colors.

#043
XL Recordings

+**Design Firm** Airside
+**Website** www.airside.co.uk
+**Client** XL Recordings

+**Creative Director** Fred Deakin
+**Designer** Airside
+**Printer/Production** Think Tank Media

In this promotional pack, each of the nine badges is decorated with individual artwork to represent the nine tracks included on the CD. Each track has an accompanying animated video on the DVD, and the badge artwork was taken from the DVD visuals. The badges are held in a die-cut, white foam insert, placed in a jewel case with a paper inlay. The unique and colorful badges gave this promotion a distinct and individual edge.

Badges. Badges! BADGES! Pin 'em on your jacket, swap 'em with your friends, pierce your nipples with them. Do what you want with them but WORSHIP THEM. And especially worship these, the first ever collection of LEMON JELLY badges featuring luverly artwork fashioned by top design bods AIRSIDE and taken from the new Lemon Jelly album/CD/ DVD/combine harvester '64 - '95 which is available in the shops NOW! Gawrsh, but life is sweet...

#044
Studio Monkeys

+**Design Firm** Studio Monkeys
+**Website** www.studio-monkeys.com
+**Client** Studio Monkeys

+**Creative Directors** Tim Longthorn, Nik Moran
+**Designers** Tim Longthorn, Nik Moran
+**Printer/Production** Print Ideas Ltd

Studio Monkeys produced its business card on GF Smith's 350gsm Colorplan black and citrine, with high-gloss black foil blocking applied to both faces of a custom-made triplexed (three sheets of 350gsm laminated together) substrate.

Studio Monkeys faced various production problems. Initially it wanted to use a four-ply card, but because no press could successfully foil block this weight, it explored the option of having the individual sheets preprinted and laminated. This proved unsuccessful owing to slippage and misregistration, so the design was changed to use a thinner, but still substantial three-ply board. The studio then had to source a printshop with a press that could foil block the laminated board.

Triplexed boards
These stunning business cards show what can be achieved if you simply ask. For this effect, three sheets of board (in two different colors) were pressed and laminated to provide a unique finish.

Perspex

Clear red Perspex, 4mm (c. ³⁄₁₆in) thick, was chosen to form the material for the discount card. As Perspex cannot be printed on using conventional methods, screen printing had to be used to get the desired results.

#045
Miss Selfridge

+**Design Firm** Design N/A
+**Website** www.design-na.co.uk
+**Client** Miss Selfridge

+**Creative Directors** Neil Emery, Adam Thorpe
+**Designer** Design N/A
+**Printer/Production** Good News Press, BEP, Hamar Acrylic Ltd.

As part of its 40th anniversary year promotions, Miss Selfridge wanted to produce a VIP discount card for a select list of fashion editors and celebrities. Design N/A produced a red luminous Perspex card, each silk screened with metallic ruby ink and individually numbered. The card was presented in a book jacket cover, printed with a special red ink, gloss laminated, and then foil blocked with a matte white "40" to the cover. The inside front cover held a booklet containing an introduction, press images, and terms and conditions. The final case was packaged in a screen-printed red padded envelope. Finishing and materials included 4mm (³⁄₁₆in) luminous red clear Perspex, 2,000 micron gray board, gloss lamination, white matte foil, screen printing, foil blocking, and book binding.

#046
Royal Bank of Scotland

+**Design Firm** Nick Clark Design
+**Website** www.nickclarkdesign.co.uk
+**Client** Royal Bank of Scotland

+**Creative Director** Nick Clark
+**Designer** Nick Clark
+**Printer/Production** Berrico Ltd.

This invitation not only involved using a 20 percent cotton, acid-free calcium carbonate buffered stock (160gsm Canaletto Grossa from R. K. Burt), but also a blowtorch, hot wax seals, a large bread knife, and unfragranced extra-strength hair spray from L'Oréal. Once printed, each invitation was hand-torn to give a rough edge, slashed on the sides with a bread knife, severely scorched with a lit blowtorch, then put out, carefully dusted down, and sealed from excessive smudging using odorless hair spray. The invitations were then hand-folded into an old-fashioned self-envelope and given a hot wax seal with a brass seal and tartan ribbon. To achieve a further level of "sinisterness," they were inserted into a tissue-lined, gusseted envelope made by a small family business in East London.

#047
Royal Bank of Scotland

+**Design Firm** Nick Clark Design
+**Website** www.nickclarkdesign.co.uk
+**Client** Royal Bank of Scotland

+**Creative Director** Nick Clark
+**Designer** Nick Clark
+**Printer/Production** Various

Nick Clark designed campaign material for the Royal Bank of Scotland to invite guests to matches at the 2006 FIFA World Cup. There were many different processes used to produce the elements of this campaign. The first element was a screen-printed "soccer pitch." The green felt was sourced from a supplier in England and sent in rolls to silk screen printers in London. The cloth was cut to size and printed one-up white silk screen, trimmed and tidied, and tagged with a die-cut radius cornered printed card. A foil-blocked gold and black label was added to the piece before sending it out in a metallic gold C4 (229 × 324mm/9 × 12¾in) envelope. The main piece of the campaign—a retro-styled "Subbuteo" box containing ten miniature scaled soccer players—was produced in China. Finishing included silk screen printing, plastic injection molding, die-cutting, kiss-cutting, hand assembly, litho printing, and foil blocking.

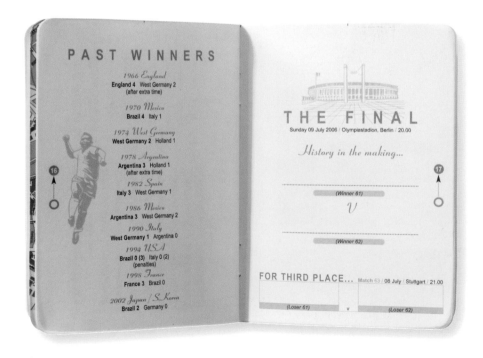

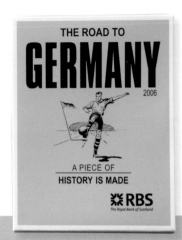

#048
EMI Records

+**Design Firm** Zip Design
+**Website** www.zipdesign.co.uk
+**Client** EMI Records

+**Creative Director** Peter Chadwick
+**Designer** Daniel Koch
+**Printer/Production** EMI arranged print

This six-page, roll-fold flyer was created to promote the launch of the new album from Beth Orton. Commissioned by the record label, and working closely with Beth herself, Zip created the full release campaign for the album and singles. This included all associated promo and marketing items. All printed parts were produced on uncoated, recycled stock to give the campaign a muted and organic feel that complemented the flavor of Beth's music. The invites and flyers that launched the campaign included the Beth Orton logo and type printed one color on a heavily textured grayboard.

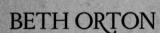

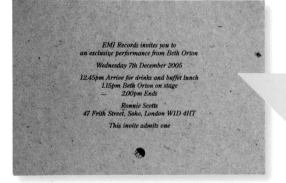

Pulp board

Pulp board, being very thick and absorbent, is incredibly difficult to print onto. Its rough texture and dense weight also help to make projects memorable.

#049
Game Paused

+**Design Firm** Serial Cut
+**Website** www.serialcut.com
+**Client** Game Paused

+**Creative Director** Sergio del Puerto
+**Designer** Sergio del Puerto
+**Printer/Production** Serial Cut

Serial Cut™ designed a collection of eight hand-painted ceramic dishes for the book and exhibition <u>Game Paused: A Creative Celebration of the Videogame</u>. A project on this theme brings to mind pixels, LED screens, and joysticks, but it can also be represented in more retro ways—Pac-Man, Mario Bros, Donkey Kong, PaperBoy, Bubble Bobble, and Sonic. The dishes have become collector pieces and realize the traditional vision of our most memorable heroes of past computer gaming.

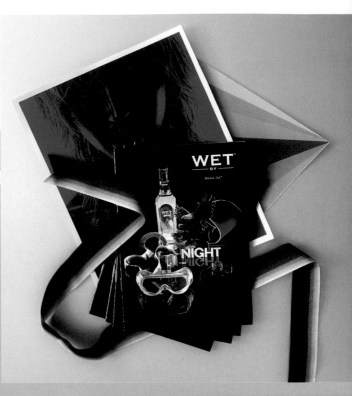

#050
WET

+**Design Firm** Serial Cut
+**Website** www.serialcut.com
+**Client** WET

+**Creative Director** Sergio del Puerto
+**Designer** Sergio del Puerto
+**Printer/Production** Graficas Deva

This is a 20-page promotional magazine for the first nondry gin in the world: WET by Beefeater. The publication was created by DressLab, designed by Albert Folch, and distributed in the coolest fashion stores and clubs. To promote this drink, in every WET issue, a creative is asked to develop an idea based on a particular theme. For the first issue, Serial Cut™ worked with the theme of "Night."

All photographed elements were real—the final result was a photographic collage, with elements that had been scanned, printed, and cut including typography made from plastic and real elements (pink strips, straws, ice cubes, glasses, diskettes, etc.). This collage could easily have been done with Photoshop, but was actually done in a photography studio, and was barely retouched digitally.

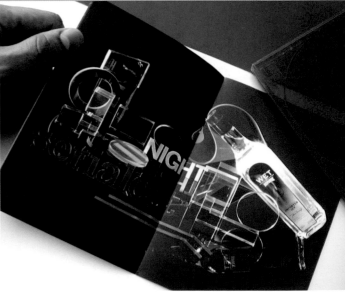

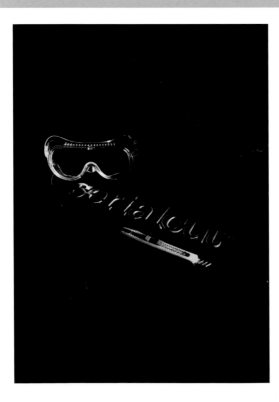

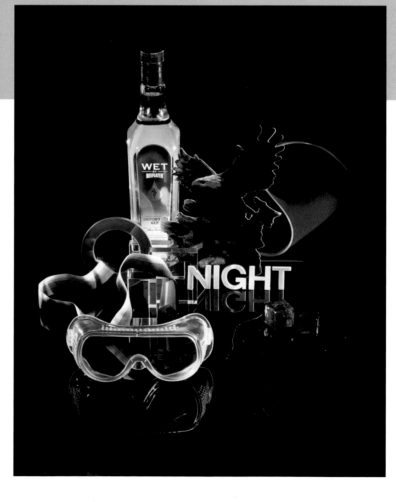

Standard Printing

#051
RCA, Miquelrius

+**Design Firm** Astrid Stavro
+**Website** www.astridstavro.com
+**Clients** Royal College of Art, Miquelrius

+**Creative Director** Astrid Stavro
+**Designers** Astrid Stavro, Birgit Pfisterer
+**Printer/Production** ALTES, S. A.

Astrid Stavro designed a series of seven different notepads that recreate grids that played a historic role in the development of design systems. These notepads cover a wide spectrum of classic and contemporary editorial design. Besides their role as historic "reminders" and homages, the notepads may be used for memo notes, doodling, shopping lists, writing letters, etc. Materials used included 100gsm Conqueror smooth ivory uncoated paper and 3,000 micron gray cardboard.

The series includes the following notepads/grids: Jan Tschichold, Le Corbusier, Willy Fleckhause, Josef Müller-Brockmann, Paul Rand, Johannes Gutenberg, and David Hillman.

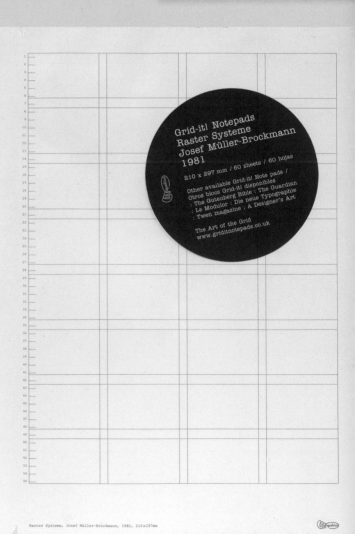

#052
Going Underground

+**Design Firm** Bleed
+**Website** www.bleed.no
+**Client** Going Underground

+**Creative Director** Kjetil World
+**Designer** Kjetil World
+**Printer/Production** Alfaprint

Bleed designed the poster, using 200gsm Arctic gloss, for the contemporary furniture fair Going Underground in Stockholm. The fair was located at a hotel parking lot and the poster reflected that idea. The poster ended up being 250cm (100in) long. The message "going underground" was then directly applied and pointed people toward the location of the event. Typography was also made out of meshed tape to create unique lettering. The same tape was used to put up the posters.

#053
Close Encounters Ypenburg

+**Design Firm** Catalogtree
+**Website** www.catalogtree.net
+**Client** Close Encounters Ypenburg

+**Creative Director** Catalogtree
+**Designers** Daniel Gross, Joris Maltha
+**Printer/Production** Albani, Plaatsmaken, HAL Zeefdruk

Close Encounters Ypenburg is an annual movie festival held on the streets of a suburb in The Hague. Catalogtree enjoyed producing its larger-format screen-printed posters. As a production technique, screen print is both restrictive and rewarding at the same time: loss in detail is counterbalanced by vibrant color. For the festival program, Catalogtree used rolitho paper. This paper is quite transparent and coated on one side. When folded into a program, the alternation of shiny and matte paper together with the see-through typography gave depth to the design.

**10 september 2005
20.30 — 24.00 uur
Festival met Film /
Video / Muziek**

**Patrijsplantsoen
Ypenburg, Den Haag
info: www.7X11.nl
toegang gratis**

Video
Jeroen Eisinga, Benny Nemerofsky,
Robert Hamilton, TRAKTOR, Michel
Gondry, Nicolas Provost, Guido van
der Werve, Jan van Nuenen e.a.

Film
Psycho (Hitchcock 1960 /
Gus van Sant 1998)

Muziek
Urbi et Orbi

Close Encounters Ypenburg 2 is een initiatief van 7X11 en Artoteek Den Haag

Monotone

This piece uses a single spot color
printing onto colored paper to
achieve strong, bold results. Tints
of the single color can add depth
and push the boundaries of what
monotone printing can achieve.

#054
Hello Duudle

+**Design Firms** Hello Duudle, Wiggleton Press
+**Website** www.helloduudle.com
+**Client** Hello Duudle

+**Creative Director** Jon Burgerman
+**Designers** Jon Burgerman, Sune Ehlers
+**Printer/Production** Wiggleton Press

This book project was the combination of a collaboration between Sune Ehlers and Jon Burgerman. They wanted the book to be enjoyed on its own merits and to act as a promotional item. The book was printed in China on 600gsm gray board coated with 128gsm art paper that was then matte laminated. A gold foil detail was added to the lid and base. A spot UV varnish was also used on the artwork.

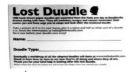

Matte laminating

Matte laminating involves bonding a matte plastic film directly to a sheet of paper using heat and pressure. Laminating protects the printed sheet and prevents the "cracking" that can occur where large areas of solid inks are printed across folds.

Kraft paper

A strong and durable paper made from unbleached wood pulp often used for paperbags and wrapping, this can also yield interesting results when used as a printing substrate.

#055
Various

+**Design Firm** Jewboy
+**Website** www.jewboy.co.il
+**Clients** Various

+**Creative Director** Jewboy
+**Designer** Jewboy
+**Printer/Production** Various

Here are various promotional works from the Tel Aviv–based designer/artist known simply as Jewboy. Working with many exciting clients in all formats of media, Jewboy's collaborations include Cronica Records Ran Slavin CD promotional postcards on 400gsm carton with matte lamination. The entire CD package design and promotion materials were made by scanning different body parts of people—clients, family, friends, etc.

Other works include the Zamir Club party poster for the "Tel Aviv's Burning Down" party. Jewboy observes, "It's funny and sad how this headline became more than accurate."

#056
Mamtor

+**Design Firm** Muller
+**Website** www.hellomuller.com
+**Client** Mamtor™ Publishing

+**Creative Director** Tom Muller
+**Designer** Tom Muller
+**Printer/Production** Brenner Printing

Mamtor: Event Horizon is a sci-fi, horror, and fantasy anthology published by Mamtor™ Publishing. The first book showcases the works of established writers and artists, as well as offering a platform for new talent to "break in" and tell their stories. Event Horizon is a creator-driven project, offering a platform for work that falls out of the mainstream: a forum for the subculture.

Materials include Cornwall and Orion Gloss with matte lamination and spot gloss varnish. The variant cover has an added fifth (metallic) color finish.

Standard lithography

The standard process of printing from a flat surface, such as a metal plate, treated so that a specific image area holds ink, which is then transferred to the receiving material. Standard litho printing is used for most projects with large print runs, including magazines and brochures.

#057
Total Content

Letterpress
A very traditional practice of printing from an inked, raised surface. In this case, using wooden blocks with an aged, damaged surface gives the range of stationery a fantastic and imperfect look and feel.

+**Design Firm** NB: Studio
+**Website** www.nbstudio.co.uk
+**Client** Total Content

+**Creative Directors** Alan Dye, Nick Finney, Ben Stott
+**Designer** Daniel Lock
+**Printer/Production** Hand & Eye Letterpress

Copywriters Total Content needed a set of new stationery. NB:Studio's design took its cue from the company name and features the total contents of a copywriter's most basic everyday tool, the alphabet. Character and punctuation symbols were placed in a variety of different fonts to reflect the different personalities and styles of Total Content's writing. All stationery items were letterpress printed to give a crafted look and feel and make each item individual. Fluro Orange was used to reflect the company's Dutch heritage.

Materials included GF Smith's 150gsm and 350gsm Colorplan Pristine White. Printing was by letterpress printing both sides in double-hit Pantone 805U 2X.

totalcontent. Studio The Abbey Warwick Road Southam Warwickshire United Kingdom CV47 0HN
T +01926 812286 M +07976 160967 F +01926 811386 jim@totalcontent.co.uk www.totalcontent.co.uk

VAT No. 796 3716 85

#058
Restaurant de Salentein

+**Design Firm** QuA Associates
+**Web** www.qua.nl
+**Client** Restaurant de Salentein

+**Creative Director** Erik Schuur
+**Designers** Verena Hauschke, Linda Voogd
+**Printer/Production** Drukkerij Kempers, Production Dept

Restaurant de Salentein is located in Nijkerk, in the Netherlands. It is part of a country estate and its aristocratic and natural surroundings formed the main influences on the visual style developed by QuA Associates. The fact that the restaurant is linked to Salentein wines (an Argentinian label) also had to be communicated. To reflect all of this, the design uses classical typography in a modern way, along with organic and natural forms taken from both the country estate and the Argentinian landscape, and forged to give a rich, but natural and fresh visual language. In addition to stationery and menus, QuA developed graphic items for the restaurant interior, including wallpaper and lampshades.

#059
J.Lindeberg

+**Design Firm** Saturday
+**Website** www.saturday-london.com
+**Client** J.Lindeberg

+**Creative Director** Erik Tarsknsson
+**Designer** Saturday
+**Printer/Production** Saturday

Saturday created the identity for J.Lindeberg's sports label Future Sports.
Based on a circle, the identity spans packaging, labeling, stores, and advertising.
Today it can be seen on some of the world's best athletes in skiing and golf,
two areas where J.Lindeberg has redefined style.

Saddle-stitching

The standard method of binding
by applying staples through the
centerfold of nested signatures. This
is the most common form of binding.

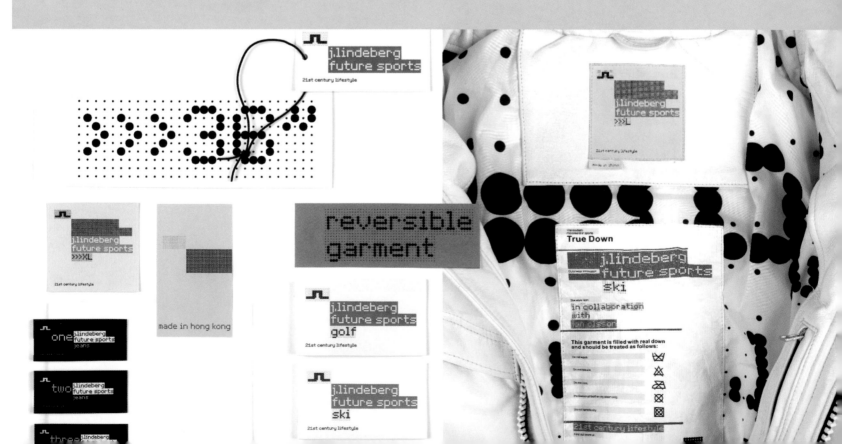

profile
camilo villegas

look as
good as your
game

Camilo Villegas on J.Lindeberg Future Sports Golf

full name_Camilo Villegas
height_5'9"
weight_142 lbs
date of birth_7.1.1982
place of birth_Medellin, Colombia
residence_Gainesville, Florida, USA;
plays out of University Golf Course, Gainesville, Florida, USA
family_Single
special interests_Soccer and fitness
turned professional_2004

career history & highlights:
Four-time All-American at the university of Florida with eight victories,
breaking the career record set by Chris DiMarco.
Turned professional in time for the 2004 U.S. Open at Shinnecock Hills.
Earned $237,984 in just 10 starts on the PGA Tour.
His best was a tie for seventh at the 2004 B.C. Open
and twelfth at the 2004 Deutsche Bank Championship.
One of the coolest new, up and coming golfers – a destined J. Lindeberg
player that looks like a modern Marlon Brando.

J.Lindeberg   www.
Future Sports Golf   jlindeberg.com

34—
35

stretch
windstopper
Outerwear collection

The Trainings

hunter aqua
miracle

#060
Tequila\Manchester

+**Design Firm** Andy Smith
+**Website** www.asmithillustration.com
+**Client** Tequila\Manchester

+**Creative Director** Andy Smith
+**Designer** Andy Smith
+**Printer/Production** The Anton Group

Andy Smith was briefed to produce a large-format promotional book that illustrates how an idea is developed and turned into creative work. The book is printed in three spot colors, with all other colors being produced by overlapping these colors. This was intended to give it a very "printy" feel. Smith recalls difficulties caused by the restrictions created by using only three spot colors, but successfully rose above these challenges. The paper choice, 430 micron Vanguard by the Paper Co., was important and gave the book a textured and heavy feel.

Large format
Printing large scale requires finding a printer with large presses capable of taking sheet sizes big enough to print the project conventionally. For conventional lithography, B1 (707 × 1,000mm/27¾ × 39⅓in) presses are among the largest.

#061
UCK

+**Design Firm** Main Studio
+**Website** www.mainstudio.com
+**Client** Utrecht Centrum voor de Kunsten

+**Creative Director** Edwin Van Gelder
+**Designer** Edwin Van Gelder
+**Photographer** Barrie Hullegie
+**Printer/Production** Culen

Main Studio designed a poster and flyer for the Amateur Theater Festival in Utrecht, the Netherlands. Eggs were used as a metaphor for the reaction of crowds confronted with a bad performance. Eggs thrown at people were photographed to create strong, poetic images. The campaign, rolled out mainly around Utrecht, consisted of two posters (A1; 594 × 841mm/ 23½ × 33in), a program booklet (A5; 148 × 210mm/5¾ × 8¼in), a leaflet (A5; 148 × 210mm/5¾ × 8¼in), and T-shirts.

Roll-fold

In roll-folding, the page is repeatedly folded, in panels or sections, from one edge toward the other. When folded out, this results in a number of "pages" being visible at the same time.

#062
Galerie Rudolfinum

+**Design Firm** Heyduk Musil Strnad
+**Website** www.hmsdesign.cz
+**Client** Galerie Rudolfinum

+**Creative Directors** Filip Heyduk, Martin Strnad
+**Designers** Filip Heyduk, Martin Strnad
+**Printer/Production** Realistic S.V.O.

This project involved the complete corporate design for an exhibition celebrating the Holland-based photographer Rineke Dijkstra. The exhibition was held in Prague. Materials for the catalog included 300gsm and 150gsm Plandplus with conventional litho printing as well as silk print.

#063

Various

+**Design Firm** You Are Beautiful
+**Web** www.youarebeautiful.co.uk
+**Clients** Various

+**Creative Director** Kerry Roper
+**Designer** Kerry Roper
+**Printer/Production** Various

Album covers are an exciting area of design. Kerry Roper of You are Beautiful believes that listening to and understanding the client's music helps provide inspiration, but, where the singer likes one thing, the drummer another, and the manager something else altogether, things can get very complicated. Roper's solution is to keep the band informed at all times during the design process, as this helps things run more smoothly. Another factor that must be considered is the various formats the designs will be used on; this artwork was used on pieces from CD size to 300mm (12in), and even on posters.

SUMMER OF SPACE with you

01/Original
02/Kaskade Does Rock Mix
03/Johnny Fiasco's Chunkafunk Mix
04/Ronan's Peak Time Dub
05/Members Only Vocal Mix
06/Leo Portela's Vocal Sunrise Mix
07/Members Only Dub
08/Kaskade Does Rock Edit
09/Original Instrumental
10/Original Radio Edit

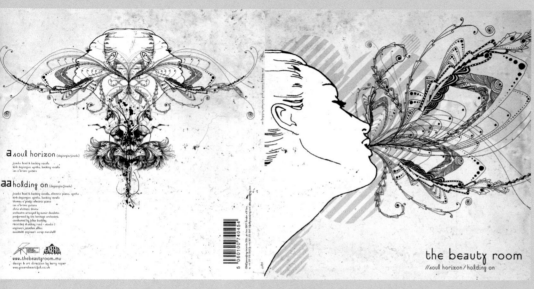

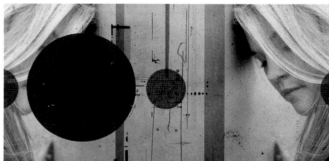

Bleed

The bleed is the printed area that extends beyond the trimmed edge of a printed document. Bleed is usually set up at the artwork stage of the design process to extend 3–5mm (⅛–¼in) over where the printer has to trim. Bleed ensures that when the printed page has been trimmed, no print is lost.

#064
Factor Design

+**Design Firm** Factor Design
+**Web** www.factordesign.com
+**Client** Factor Design, Inc.

+**Creative Director** Jeff Zwerner
+**Designers** Craig Williamson, Gabe Campodonica
+**Printer/Production** Cenveo

The Factor Design promotional brochure was designed to introduce and inform prospective clients of the capabilities and values of this strategic design firm. The brochure is divided into three distinct sections which address the challenges inherent in successfully launching, sustaining, or altering the course of most businesses. The sections detail Factor Design's role in launching a new product or company, renewing an existing brand, and envisioning new ways that companies use design to compete and win.

Factor used Arjo Wiggins Curious Touch Soft Milk and Mohawk Options True White Smooth in creating the brochure. Using the Curious Touch cover stock posed many initial concerns for Factor, but in the end everything worked out beautifully due to precautionary measures taken at the earliest stages of printing to stop the ultra-soft cover material from getting damaged.

#065
wake me up at

+**Design Firm** I Saw It First
+**Website** www.wakemeupat.com
+**Client** wake me up at™

+**Creative Director** I Saw It First
+**Designers** Alice Tonge, Cathy Hutton
+**Printer/Production** RochaPrint Solutions

If you frequently fall asleep on the London Underground, creatives Alice Tonge and Cathy Hutton have designed a nifty way to make sure you get to your destination. It comes in the form of a sticker set—wake me up at™—that should be in every Londoner's briefcase. Simply peel the desired stop you wish to be woken up at and stick to your jacket.

The labels were created using a matte stock and bespoke cutter guide. For the backing card, a bright white 250gsm Lumisilk was used and packaged in a bespoke polypropylene sealable bag.

Kiss-cut

Kiss-cutting is a precise form of die-cutting, perfect for the creation of sticker sheets such as this one. The die is so precise, it cuts the printed layer, but not the backing sheet.

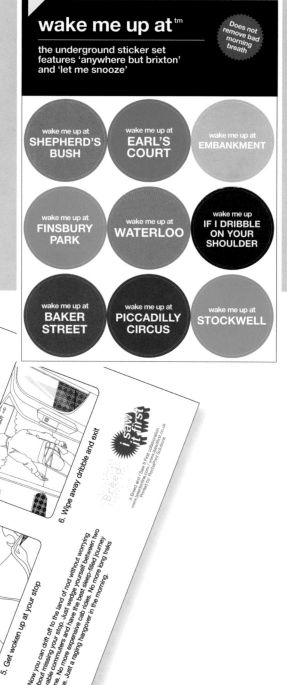

#066
Landcove Ayr

+**Design Firm** Stand
+**Website** www.stand-united.co.uk
+**Client** Landcove Ayr

+**Creative Director** Stuart Gilmour
+**Designer** Emlyn Firth
+**Printer/Production** J Thomson Colour Printers

Stand designed a brochure to promote a new property development in the west end of Glasgow, Scotland. A unique selling point of the apartments was the inclusion of a selection of highly decorative wallpapers from Scottish interior designers Timorous Beasties. The screen-printed patterns became the main features throughout the brochure and also inspired the illustration style. The brochure was printed on Think from Howard Smith using conventional CMYK litho with extra spot varnish.

Allover spot UV

Allover UVs are applied in the same manner as standard spot UVs, but cover a far greater area. They require careful attention at the printing stage to ensure that the UV is applied flat, does not bubble, and is dry before folding and finishing.

#067
Tone

+**Design Firm** Tone
+**Website** www.tonedesign.co.uk
+**Client** Tone

+**Creative Director** Tony Phillips
+**Designer** Tony Phillips
+**Printer/Production** Generation Press

The artwork for the imagery was created in negative on the reverse so that it appeared properly when printed in silver on the black material (GF Smith's 270gsm Colorplan Black). Once a negative of each image had been produced, the background had to be removed to create the desired effect. Generation Press helped Tone to realize the effect as it was impossible to visualize the final piece using its studio-based laser and inkjet printers.

Spot silver on black

Printing a spot silver directly onto black card by conventional litho can give stunning results. Here Tone has utilized the silver's opacity, allowing more of the black to shine through.

Mixing spot colors

To create an unusual black finish, Tone asked Generation Press to mix a spot silver metallic ink in with the black ink. This created a dense "super" black with a metallic sheen.

#068

Mitchell Conner Searson

+**Design Firm** Tone
+**Website** www.tonedesign.co.uk
+**Client** Mitchell Conner Searson

+**Creative Director** Tony Phillips
+**Designer** Tony Phillips
+**Printer/Production** Generation Press

For the Mitchell Conner Searson events mailers, Tone used two techniques to create a more sophisticated feel to a simple print job with a limited budget. To create more "depth" to the printed piece, Generation Press added silver ink to the black for the background color. Married with the choice of an uncoated stock, this gave a great feel to the finished mailers. Tone also created a line screen for some of the graphic elements to create the illusion of a third color without having to use a tint.

The mailers were printed on Fedrigoni's 340gsm Splendorgel in two spot colors with a metallic black background created by adding silver to black ink.

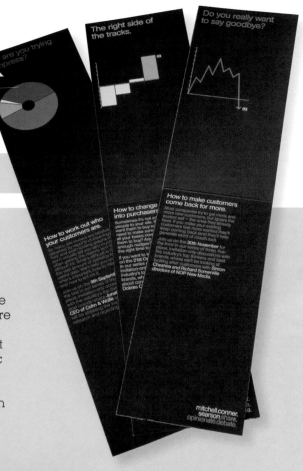

#069
Is Not Magazine

+**Design Firm** Underware
+**Website** www.underware.nl
+**Client** Is Not Magazine

+**Creative Director** Bas Jacobs
+**Designer** Underware
+**Printer/Production** Underware

Is Not take-away #01, the first collaborative project to emerge from the year-long association between Underware and Is Not Magazine, is the first portable issue of Is Not Magazine, the huge poster magazine from Melbourne that uses only Underware typefaces. It is also the comprehensive type sampler from Underware, showing its fonts in use and indexed. Underware was founded in 1999 and exists between The Hague, Helsinki, and Amsterdam. Its adventurous and well-crafted typefaces have featured in books, magazines, newspapers, posters, animations, T-shirts, signage systems, exhibitions, packaging, and even tattoos.

Monoprint

A classic example of excellent design using the cheapest possible methods of reproduction (photocopying) to achieve outstanding results.

#070
One Club

+**Design Firm** Iamalwayshungry
+**Website** www.iamalwayshungry.com
+**Client** One Club

+**Creative Director** Nessim Higson
+**Designers** Nessim Higson, John Finnell
+**Printer/Production** Iamalwayshungry

The One Club of New York approached Iamalwayshungry to create a poster for the upcoming show "Peace" and let the designers decide the poster's theme as well as its size and overall format. With the sheer amount of material President Bush has created, they chose to make him the voice of the piece, utilizing a whole side for quotes primarily attributed to him.

Iamalwayshungry printed a limited run on a thick stock and actually decided to print the remainder on a cheaper thinner stock found at the local copy/mail center.

Specialist Printing

#071
Levi Strauss Nordic

+**Design Firm** Bleed
+**Website** www.bleed.com
+**Client** Levi Strauss Nordic

+**Creative Director** Kjetil World
+**Designer** Miriam Skovholt
+**Printer/Production** Printhouse AS

Bleed created an identity for Levi Strauss Nordic to use on all its press material. The profile reflected the company's longevity with denim and customization for personal need. It also had quite a clean expression to link subconsciously to the Scandinavian lifestyle. Its specially designed font was made up of sewing needles. The letters look as though they are sewn onto the paper, and every item has descriptive words printed on with elaborate patterns of thread. The Levi's logo is foil blocked on each postal element to add to the exclusivity of the smooth paper finish (300gsm Munken Pure) and detailed print.

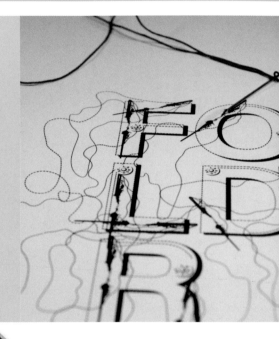

#072
Print Library

+**Design Firms** nothingdiluted studios, Hurson
+**Websites** www.nothingdiluted.com
+**Client** Print Library

+**Creative Directors** Grant Dickson, Ciaran Hurson
+**Designers** nothingdiluted studios, Hurson
+**Printer/Production** Print Library

Print Library asked nothingdiluted to create a book to demonstrate its absolute command of printing and to be a print showcase for its exceptional skills.

The book was produced using many techniques, with the title debossed on the cover with a magenta foil-blocked subheading. The book utilizes four-color process, fluorescent inks and matte/gloss varnishes, die-cuts, overprinting, and unique embossing. McNaughton paper stocks (both coated and uncoated in various weights) were used throughout the book, which was perfect bound. Overall this magnificent piece of work took a year to produce from start to finish.

Slipcase

The brochure is housed in a solid, protective, printed card slipcase. The recipient then tears open the slipcase using the kiss-cut strip on the back.

#073
Design N/A

+**Design Firm** Design N/A
+**Website** www.design-na.co.uk
+**Client** Design N/A

+**Creative Directors** Neil Emery, Adam Thorpe
+**Designer** Design N/A
+**Printer/Production** Neil Emery, Adam Thorpe

This self-promotional book was hand-printed by the creative directors of N/A. The book contains eclectic and random imagery created from N/A's photography and collected ephemera. Once the landscape format of each design had been screen printed, the book was assembled utilizing French-folds to allow each design to face another, creating a more random composition. The book was then bound with mustard book cloth on the spine and a heavy gray board cover, debossed with the N/A logo, adhered to the front and back.

Materials used included 170gsm Dutchman from ISTD Fine Paper Ltd. and 2,000 micron grayboard with Ratchfords Windsor tissue-lined cloth finished using screen printing and debossing.

Binding tape
To bind this book a mustard-colored book cloth was applied to both cover and spine. The outer card cover was then glued to complete the front and back of the brochure.

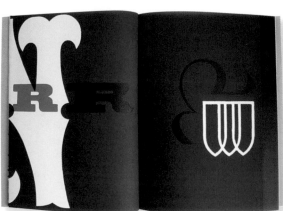

#074

Ryan Burlinson

+**Design Firm** Ryan Burlinson
+**Website** www.wolkencommunica.com
+**Client** Ryan Burlinson

+**Creative Director** Ryan Burlinson
+**Designer** Ryan Burlinson
+**Printer/Production** Evolution Press

Burlinson produced his own 2-color wedding invite combining professional letterpress with simple laser and inkjet printing. Being on a tight budget, Burlinson focused mostly on the invite card. With a short run of 250, he was able to accomplish many elements himself—the blind embossed logo was achieved with a very inexpensive hand-stamp embosser. Chocolate-brown envelopes were altered and created using a homemade die.

#075
Cycling England

+**Design Firm** Heard Creative
+**Website** www.heardcreative.co.uk
+**Client** Cycling England

+**Creative Director** Tim Heard
+**Designer** Simon Collins
+**Printer/Production** Vertec Printing, Thin Air

Bikeability is a new cycling award scheme in England designed to give children the necessary skills to cycle safely on today's modern roads. The Bikeability Award itself consists of a fluorescent metal nickel badge, information booklet, and certificate all contained within a presentation folder.

Finishing included screen printing, litho printing, and badge manufacturing, with fluorescent inks used throughout. Materials included enamel-plated nickel badges, polypropylene folders, and matte-coated stock for the booklets (Chromomatt paper).

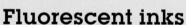

Fluorescent inks
More opaque and vibrant than standard inks, fluorescents can be mixed with process inks to increase their vibrancy. However, fluorescent inks can fade if left in strong sunlight.

wicked!
You've just pedalled your way to success and proved your Bikeability!

#076
Amrita & Mallika

+**Design Firm** Spin
+**Website** www.spin.co.uk
+**Client** Amrita & Mallika

+**Creative Director** Tony Brook
+**Designer** Spin
+**Printer/Production** Benwell Sebard

Amrita & Mallika wanted a feminine identity that celebrated their individuality. Spin adapted American Typewriter, an elegant and classic slab-serif font, to create a decorative logotype and fused this with the vibrant colors of Bombay. All the type was foil blocked with the logotype foiled in silver. The insides of the folders and envelopes were all in one of the colors from the palette. The result was a lively, distinct, and personal identity that had its roots in India but maintains an international appeal. Materials included Colorplan (single sheets and duplexed sheeted) and Accent Smooth from GF Smith.

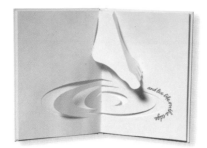

#077

MAP Financial Services

+**Design Firm** Voice
+**Website** www.voicedesign.net
+**Client** MAP Financial Services

+**Creative Directors** Scott Carslake, Stuart Gluth
+**Designers** Scott Carslake, Stuart Gluth
+**Printer/Production** Regal Printing

MAP Financial Services asked Voice to design a standard A4 (210 × 297mm/8¼ × 11¾in) brochure to promote its financial planning business. However, Voice soon discovered that MAP actually needed a unique item to make it more memorable with potential customers.

As MAP develops financial solutions that are specifically dictated by its customers' lifestyle choices, the design used the pop-up book medium coupled with simple rhyming verses to stimulate imagination and encourage memorability through interactivity. The book was produced all in white to give the viewer free rein to take this story and make it their own.

Pop-ups

Pop-ups can be created by die-cutting pages, but, instead of fully removing the die-cut section, adding scoring and folding against the natural direction of the folded pages. When the page is opened, the pop-up will leap out.

#078
Andy Smith

+**Design Firm** Andy Smith
+**Website** www.asmithillustration.com
+**Client** Andy Smith

+**Creative Director** Andy Smith
+**Designer** Andy Smith
+**Printer/Production** Andy Smith

Andy Smith used hand-drawn lettering and fonts in this self-promotional book to promote his hand-drawing typography. The book was hand-printed in a limited edition of 300. It was screen printed in one matte ink and one gloss ink on 100 percent recycled 170gsm Cyclus Offset paper.

#079
Abu Dhabi Tourism Authority

Black foil blocking

This stunning invitation uses several techniques in its finishing. Perhaps the most interesting, yet understated, is the use of a black foil blocking on black card, with fantastic results.

+**Design Firm** Four IV
+**Website** www.fouriv.com
+**Client** Abu Dhabi Tourism Authority

+**Creative Director** Andy Bone
+**Designer** Oliver Ellis
+**Printer/Production** Benwell Sebard

This invitation was designed by London's Four IV for the Abu Dhabi Tourism Authority for the opening of its UK office. The invitation was printed using gloss UV, black foil, and gold foil on GF Smith's 135gsm and 540gsm Colorplan Ebony.

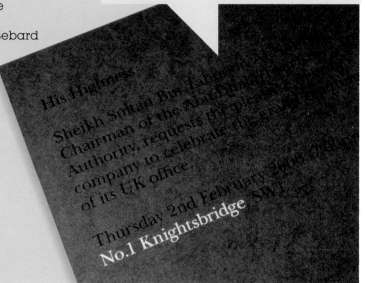

#080
Philippe Archontakis

+**Design Firm** Philippe Archontakis
+**Website** www.philippearchontakis.com
+**Client** Philippe Archontakis

+**Creative Director** Philippe Archontakis
+**Designer** Philippe Archontakis
+**Printer/Production** Boulanger Printing

Canadian designer Philippe Archontakis explored different print finishes
in creating a timeless piece of promotional graphics for his own website.
The clean and typographical approach adopted by Archontakis is
indicative of the designer's fresh take on layouts and belief that "less"
is truly always "more."

This classy finish was achieved by hot-foil stamping a single spot black
onto a Midnight Black/Brilliant White 130C Duplex from the Pegasus range
by Fraser Papers.

#081
Carnyx Group

+**Design Firm** Traffic DC
+**Website** www.traffic-design.co.uk
+**Client** Carnyx Group

+**Creative Director** Scott Witham
+**Designers** Chris Smith, Gordon Beveridge,Stephen Kelman
+**Printer/Production** Beith Printing

The Carnyx Group approached Glasgow-based design consultants Traffic to design its 2005 Drum Yearbook. The Yearbook promotes the creativity and achievements of Scottish media companies from design through to PR and photographers. The Carnyx Group wanted a highly unusual cover treatment that would not exceed the budget. Working closely with Beith Printing, Traffic chose to lay down a flat cyan to overprint the black (creating a super black). Beith Printing matte laminated the cover, but overheated the laminate to cause a stressed lamination that was then overprinted with a spot UV varnish.

Stressed lamination
Stressed lamination involves overheating the laminate before it has had time to dry fully. This process can yield very different results depending on the stock, heat, and conditions applied.

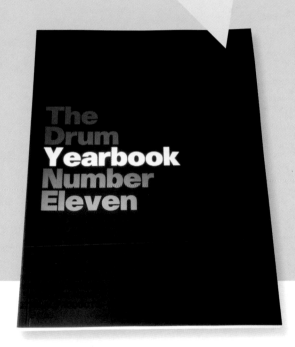

#082
Kunstencentrum Belgie

+**Design Firm** Sound in Motion
+**Client** Kunstencentrum Belgie

+**Creative Director** Cools Pascal
+**Designer** Cools Pascal
+**Printer/Production** Vuye Printers

Sound in Motion was commissioned by Kunstencentrum Belgie, an arts center located in a building once used for importing and distributing colonial goods in the 1930s. "Distribution" was its inspiration for the 2005 arts festival; it used brown wrapping paper and labels with metallic colors to create contrast.

For the 2006 festival, designer Cools Pascal changed direction by creating a 3-D poster design. This involved Pascal wearing 3-D glasses throughout the creation of the project.

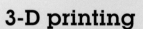

3-D printing

This complex process is difficult to get right. The background layer has to be oversized, layers that will be on similar depth planes grouped together, and different combinations of the animation layers must be exported to create the viewing angles. Special rounding effects can also be added for extra realism. Only then is the work ready to print as a 3-D animation.

Mixing stock

With these posters an interesting effect has been created by mixing a coarse brown wrapping paper with a strong white silk paper, which is printed and glued directly to the backing paper.

#083
Apt. 164

+**Design Firm** Thoughtomatic
+**Website** www.thoughtomatic.co.uk
+**Client** Apt. 164

+**Creative Directors** David Cole, John Gavin
+**Designers** David Cole, John Gavin
+**Printer/Production** G&B Printers

On viewing this unique luxury development, potential buyers were given an equally unique brochure to remind them of the experience. Thoughtomatic's landscape format gave an impression of what it was like to stand inside the space, while the three-page throw-out showed the incredible unobscured views over London. The colors used were inspired by the interior and reflected finishes found within the apartment. The cover used a black-on-black effect with a panoramic skyline view, applied using a specially spruced foil from Germany that wrapped around the entire front and back cover.

A matte-coated stock countered the heavy ink coverage inside the brochure, and a cyan tint was added to give the richest possible black. Metallic ink and gloss UV varnish were used to add luster and depth.

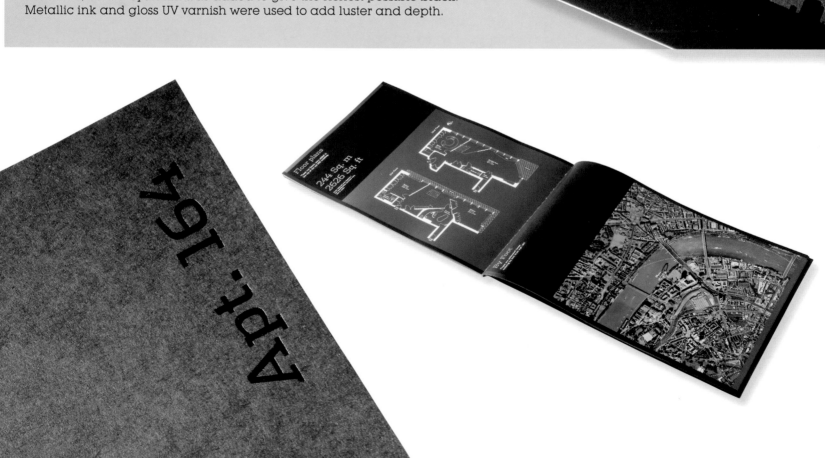

The old commission system is no more.

Some of our competitors milked it to death.

If IFAs didn't exist...

#084
DM Leslie & Pentleton

+**Design Firm** Whitespace
+**Website** www.whitespacers.com
+**Client** DM Leslie & Pentleton

+**Creative Director** Ian Valentine
+**Designers** Claire Morrow, Daniel Freitag, Ben Morris, Chris Miller
+**Printer/Production** Beith Printing

DM Leslie & Pentleton, an Edinburgh-based independent financial advisor, took the bold move to explain, within a printed brochure, people's preconceptions of IFAs. These formed the basis of a brochure targeted at solicitors, accountants, and other business introducers. The humorous approach of the brochure prompted an incredibly warm reaction.

Stock used included Dutch unlined grayboard, with foil blocking and two spot colors throughout.

who would timeshare salesmen look down on?

Board cover

For the cover of this brochure, Dutch, unlined grayboard was used for the front and back, with a silver foil blocking applied to the card. The final result is a substantial and solid-feeling document.

Alas, poor cash cow.
Toupees and spectacles have been flying in all directions. There's been quite a shake-up in the industry. Our regulatory body, the FSA, has laid down new directives. These will bring about major improvements, including greater accountability. Clients will now know exactly what they'll be paying. And complaints will be handled much more straightforwardly.

Commission: impossible?
Well, not exactly. Commission will still exist, but the emphasis now lies squarely on fees. IFAs have to offer a clear fee option to their clients. So the days of hefty hidden charges are over. Which is why the number of our less reputable competitors is set to plummet. Mainly, we'd imagine, from upper-storey window ledges. We recommend you invest in a sturdy umbrella.

An IFA without independence is worth FA.

If IFAs didn't exist...

#085
Teague

+**Design Firm** Turnstyle
+**Website** www.turnstylestudio.com
+**Client** Teague

+**Creative Directors** Ben Graham, Steve Watson
+**Designers** Ben Graham, Steve Watson, Jason Gómez, Bryan Mamaril
+**Printer/Production** Blanchette Press, Graphic Impressions

This limited edition (1,000) of <u>Design This Day: 8 Decades of Influential Design</u> was created to commemorate Teague's 80th anniversary while acknowledging W.D. Teague's book of the same title (<u>Design This Day</u>, 1940). It is a compilation of Teague's work and its perspective on the industry's most inspired, thoughtful, striking, and even amusing designs.

The book comes within an off-white cardboard Fibre Mark Touché packaging adorned with a foil stamp, opaque white, gloss black, and blind embossing. Its cover is on a Pegasus Vellum Midnight Black stock. Its interior was printed in offset CMYK and two PMS (Pantone matching system) with spot varnishing and an overall aqueous coating across a multitude of stocks. These included Domtar Luna Matte and Luna Gloss, UV Ultra II, (White), Neenah (Eames, Graphite), and Carnival Vellum Ice.

Mixing finishes

In this example, several special finishes have been used together on the same page. The tactile stock used on the cover has an unusual feel. Foil stamp, opaque white, gloss black, and blind embossing are all used.

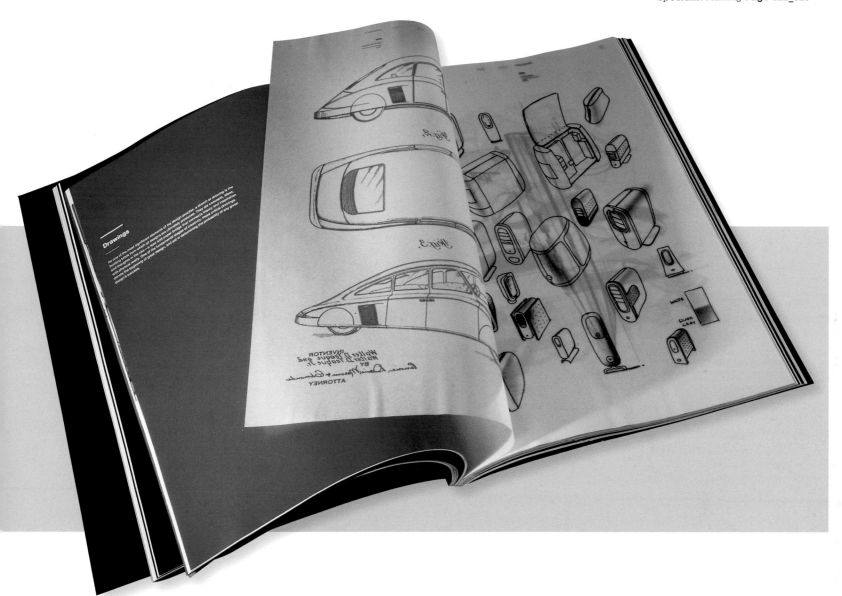

Drawings

As one of the most significant elements of the design process, a sketch or drawing is the starting point from which all designs are ultimately shaped. They are concepts, ideas, and thoughts in the raw. One of the fundamental stages of creativity, these critical drawings encourage beneficial competition, and aid in determining the practicality of any given design's success.

GET TO KNOW YOUR EGO

All designers have egos. They're a necessary tool of the trade. Our egos propel us forward, encourage beneficial competition, and are often found responsible for the exciting, breakthrough work in our field. Keep your ego sharp and intact. Learn to seek it out and nurture it in others. When used wisely, ego will lead you and your team to great things.

BECOME ADDICTED TO TALENT

Design begins and ends with talent. It's inspirational. It's refreshing. It takes us to new heights and pushes industry standards and perceptions forward. Talent is, however, greater than design. It takes talent to cultivate relationships. It takes talent to see through the "forest" of impossible and conflicting demands. It takes talent to build and lead a multicultural team. Seek out talent and pursue it at (almost) all costs.

New Domesticity

Following World War I, the financial gap between the middle and working classes shrank dramatically, with fewer and fewer American families able to afford assistance with household tasks, women began to seek new tools to streamline the most basic of domestic chores. This new demand stimulated rapid growth in the household goods market with a plethora of new devices, such as vacuum cleaners, washing machines, floor polishers, and rudimentary dishwashers becoming a staple place in American homes.

#086
Land Securities

+**Design Firm** Radford Wallis
+**Web** www.radfordwallis.com
+**Client** Land Securities

+**Creative Director** Stuart Radford, Andrew Wallis
+**Designer** Stuart Radford
+**Printer/Production** Boss Print

Land Securities commissioned Radford Wallis to design a brochure to market One Wood Street office developments. The cover, which used die-cut, duplexed Colorplan paper, is a graphic interpretation of the front elevation of the building. Inside, at the front of the brochure, this die-cut theme highlights certain design and architectural considerations. At the back, a die-cut window is used to communicate the diverse range of amenities in the area. Materials included GF Smith Colorplan Mist 2,100gsm and 175gsm, Fenner Omniar 150gsm, and James McNaughton's Challenger Laser 80gsm, with die-cut, duplexing, foil blocking, and thread-sewn finishing.

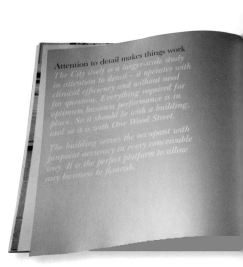

Die-cut bonding

This fantastic cover was created by foil blocking onto thick board, then die-cutting a matching stock and bonding directly on top of the printed board.

#087
Deuce Design

+**Design Firm** Deuce Design
+**Web** www.deucedesign.com.au
+**Client** Deuce Design

+**Creative Director** Bruce Slorach
+**Designer** Deuce Design
+**Printer/Production** Bruce Slorach, Alastar Spiers

This self-promotional literature for Australian Deuce Design was created to reflect the vibe and aesthetics of the studio. There are eight different business cards (for the eight members of staff) which, when turned over, complete a puzzle featuring icons that represent the business. The fluoro boxboard cover is used to contain the project sheets and send material out to clients. The exterior was left blank for plastering with stickers. Recycled, unlined boxboard, 450gsm, was screen printed in 2 colors: fluoro orange and white. The business cards and stationery were printed on Freelife Vellum, 320gsm and 120gsm respectively, with 3PMS fluoro and black matte machine varnish on two sides, and the stickers on KW Doggett pre-cut white gloss, with 1PMS fluoro 811C and black.

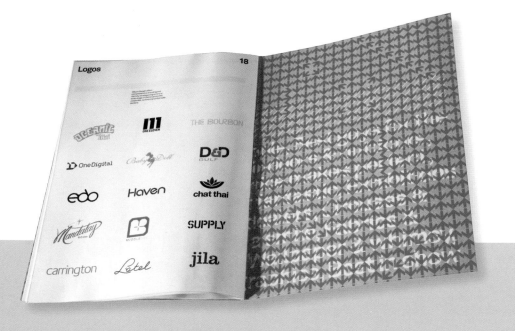

Overprinting

Overprinting onto preprinted and dried sheets creates this interesting, multilayered finish. There appears to be showthrough from the first layer of print, and this allows for the underlying text to still be legible.

#088
Rankin

+**Design Firm** BB/Saunders
+**Website** www.bbsaunders.com
+**Client** Rankin

+**Creative Director** Warren Beeby
+**Designer** Warren Beeby
+**Printer/Production** Butler and Tanner

BB/Saunders' lavish limited-edition book for Rankin, <u>Fashion Stories</u>, showcases the photographer's fashion imagery from 2005 to 2006. To create the desired expensive and luxurious feel, Creative Director Warren Beeby has applied a high-gloss UV varnish throughout. In addition, all the text is reversed out of the varnish revealing the matte of the paper underneath.

Gloss over matte

The clever and exuberant use of gloss varnish by BB/Saunders really is something special. Huge areas of the brochure are printed with gloss varnish, which is also used very subtly to create text on a matte surface.

#089
Graham Roxburgh (HfaAL)

+**Design Firm** Form
+**Website** www.form.uk.com
+**Client** Graham Roxburgh

+**Creative Directors** Paula Benson, Paul West
+**Designers** Paul West, Paula Benson, Tom Hutchings
+**Printer/Production** Granite Colour Ltd.

Form created this piece detailing the realization of a Charles Rennie
Mackintosh design to house the museum/heritage center House For
an Art Lover (HfaAL) in Glasgow, Scotland. The book promotes the
building as a museum, and as a venue for weddings, theatrical
shows, concerts, and business meetings.

Form gave the cover's striking photography an extra dimension by
using foil-blocked type. The foil-blocking process had to be monitored
carefully as any slight misalignment would have affected the design.
For the covers, 150gsm was wrapped over 2,000 micron grayboard
and matte laminated. Other materials included 160gsm Splendorgel
EW paper for the text and Think Bright for the endpapers, which were
also treated with a special silver.

#090
Form

+**Design Firm** Form
+**Website** www.form.uk.com
+**Client** Form

+**Creative Directors** Paula Benson, Paul West
+**Designers** Paula Benson, Paul West, Nick Hard
+**Printer/Production** Various

In promoting itself, Form explored different textures to take the work beyond the boundaries of paper stocks. Its brochure had to be portable, robust, and light enough to be mailed without incurring hefty postage costs. It used polypropylene, with a silver screen print and die-cut holes replicating the Form logo, because card, no matter how well treated, would show the signs of decay over a period of time.

The business cards were made from recycled sheet steel. Both sides were etched in order to cut through the circles on one side and etch the type with precision on the other.

Form®
47 Tabernacle Street
London EC2A 4AA, UK
Telephone: +44 (0)20 7014 1430
Fax: +44 (0)20 7014 1431
ISDN: +44 (0)20 7014 1432
Email: studio@form.uk.com
Web: www.form.uk.com

Acid etching

Acid etching chemically reduces the surface of a metal sheet in a controlled manner—a mask or film is bonded to the areas that must resist the chemical attack once it is applied.

Folding and Binding

#091
UBS

+**Design Firm** BB/Saunders
+**Website** www.bbsaunders.com
+**Client** UBS

+**Creative Director** Warren Beeby
+**Designer** Phil Evans
+**Printer/Production** G&B Printers

BB/Saunders produced a range of support material for UBS Openings, a wide-reaching program focused on the Tate Modern Collection. These included an invitation, RSVP, admission card, program of events, and gift. It used layered illustrations of cherry blossom, printed lithographically and with silk screen, together with unusual folding mechanisms to reflect the themes of the event, which were opening up art and the time of year (spring).

The invitation card and RSVP were mailed in an envelope that was sealed with a complex origami fold. The invitation, RSVP, admission card, program, and gift box were all screen printed with white. This overprinted the green with a semitransparent layer. All materials were printed on various weights of Think Warm from Howard Smith.

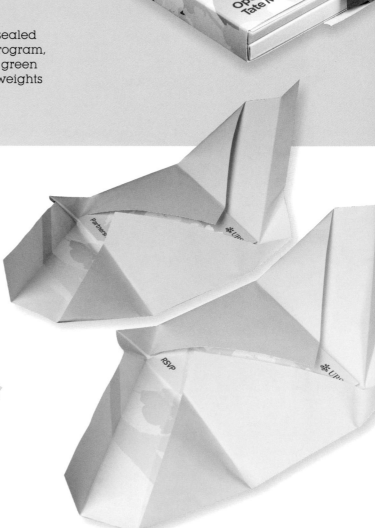

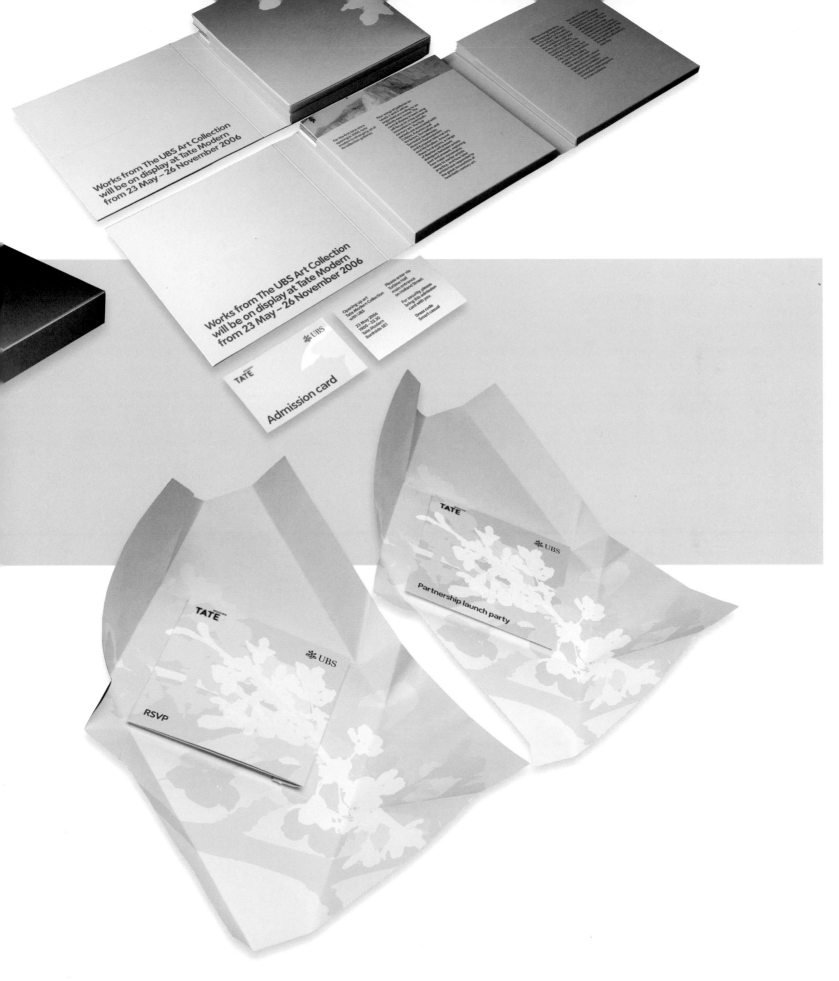

#092
Departures

+**Design Firm** Departures
+**Website** www.departuresdesign.com
+**Client** Departures

+**Creative Director** Aled Phillips
+**Designer** Aled Phillips
+**Printer/Production** Allens

Cardiff design firm Departures took inspiration from its own name for this self-promotional booklet that pays homage to retro airport information graphics. The language of the booklet is simple, effective, and direct—as is the design, printed with a single spot black on a 135gsm offset from Howard Smith. The spine of the booklet is sewn with yellow thread.

Thread sewing
Machine-sewn thread runs down the matte pages to add to the already rich and sensual feeling of this brochure. A machine varnish has also been applied to all pages to seal the color onto the paper.

We understand that each client is different; what works for one client,

...doesn't necessarily work for another.

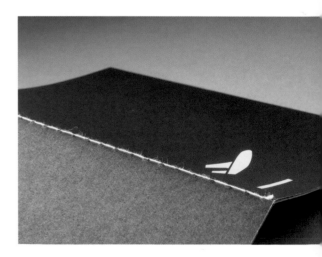

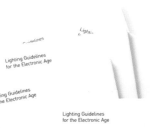

#093
Future Designs

+**Design Firm** Dowling Design & Art Direction
+**Web** www.dowlingdesign.com
+**Client** Future Designs

+**Creative Director** John Dowling
+**Designer** John Dowling
+**Printer/Production** Gavin Martin Associates

Future Designs provide both standard and bespoke lighting systems. The new Future Designs identity reflects the nature of their business and was applied across corporate stationery, direct mailings, and promotional literature including three feature booklets. Each booklet has a 4-page cover, with an additional 8-page dust jacket (plus text pages), all bound using either center sewing or three-hole sewing.

Materials used include Colorset Nero 120gsm and 270gsm, Neptune Unique 135gsm, and Colorset Solar 270gsm by Fenner Paper. Finishing included screen printing, spot litho printing, 3-hole sewing with yellow thread, and 4-color litho printing.

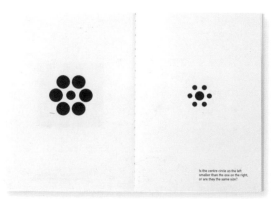

#094
Ophini Entertainment

+**Design Firm** Märang
+**Website** www.marang.com
+**Client** Ophini Entertainment

+**Creative Director** Henrik Persson
+**Designer** Märang
+**Printer/Production** Partner Print Sweden

Märang's media promotion package for a TV series about cooking and traveling in Sweden consists of a foldout cover containing a 20-page booklet and DVD. The whole media package is sealed in plastic. The thick cover folds up into a poster illustration with the DVD and booklet attached to its reverse. The DVD sits in a pocket and the booklet's last page is glued to the back of the cover.

The packaging cover was screen printed with a single black on 350gsm matte uncoated stiff paper, while the inner booklet used CMYK on 130gsm coated paper.

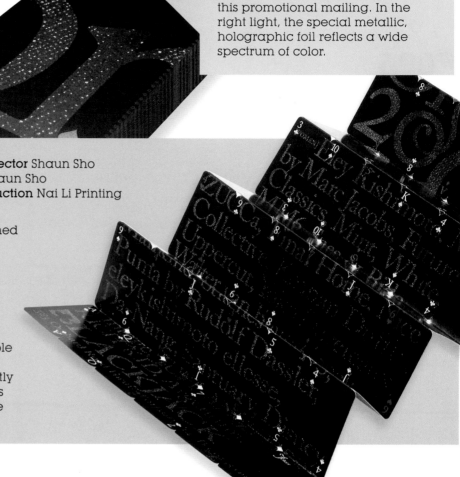

Holographic foil

Foil blocking is used throughout this promotional mailing. In the right light, the special metallic, holographic foil reflects a wide spectrum of color.

#095
BlackJack

+**Design Firm** Neighbor
+**Website** www.neighbor.com.sg
+**Clients** Club 21, BlackJack

+**Creative Director** Shaun Sho
+**Designer** Shaun Sho
+**Printer/Production** Nai Li Printing

Leading Singapore fashion boutique BlackJack approached Neighbor to design a direct mailer to promote its spring/ summer collection 2005. Drawing inspiration from the BlackJack name and its parent group Club 21, Neighbor produced the mailer as a folded poster with the stylized brand names emblazoned across the uncut sheet of 54 playing cards printed on a 300gsm art board.

After a tense production period, the combination of multiple inks and overprinting on fluorescent colors resulted in an extraordinarily well-finished project. Neighbor subsequently produced a limited edition of full-sized playing card decks that were distributed in a handsome black varnished case to 500 selected customers.

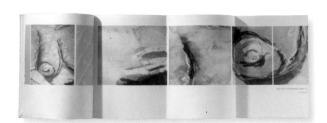

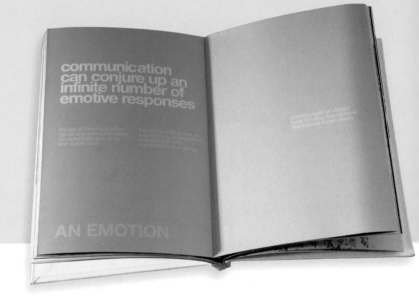

#096
Studio Locaso

+**Design Firm** Studio Locaso
+**Website** www.studiolocaso.com.au
+**Client** Studio Locaso

+**Creative Director** Patricia Locaso
+**Designers** Patricia Locaso, Jarrod Bransden
+**Printer/Production** aprint p/l, Irwin & Mclaren bookbinders

Studio Locaso's <u>Expressions</u> is a visual diary that encourages people to get their hands dirty when it comes to design. Studio Locaso's aim was to express itself using a variety of design techniques and mediums, resulting in a beautifully presented, emotive, and evocative visual diary.

The diary was printed using CMYK and PMS 319 on 135gsm Sovereign offset. It contains gatefolds, roll-folds, and an overall varnish throughout. Its hard cover is white buckram with a Japanese binding and it was packaged in a white bubble-wrap envelope.

Throw-outs

Studio Locaso inserted folded, large-format pages within this document. Known as throw-outs, these extra pages add visual interest to the brochure and allow larger surface areas for graphics.

#097

Iguatemi Shopping Mall

+**Design Firm** Superbacana Design
+**Website** www.superbacanadesign.com.br
+**Client** Iguatemi Shopping Mall

+**Creative Director** Vivian de Cerqeira Leite
+**Designers** Circe Bernardes, Gustavo Perucci
+**Printer/Production** inside: Gráficos Burti; case and cover: Papel Meoda

Brazilian firm Superbacana Design created the company prospectus for Iguatemi Shopping Mall in its hometown of São Paulo. The brochure showcased the market potential of luxury goods in the world's second largest metropolitan area.

The outer case and cover of the piece were produced on Setalux (a premium bookbinding cloth) while the text pages were on 150gsm Couchê Fosco.

Cloth outer cover

This dust jacket/sleeve was formed by bonding a high-quality black cloth onto a very heavy board. This gives the booklet a feeling similar to that of a casebound volume.

#098
Vila Naiá-Corumbau

+**Design Firm** Superbacana Design
+**Website** www.superbacanadesign.com.br
+**Client** Vila Naiá-Corumbau

+**Creative Director** Vivian de Cerqueira Leite
+**Designers** Circe Bernardes, Nina Ghellere
+**Printer/Production** J. Duarte Serigrafia, Gráfica Copibrasa, Associação Comunitária Monte Azul

Superbacana Design created this unique folder to publicize the Hotel-Pousada Vila Naiá-Corumbau in Bahia. It is packaged in a handmade white wooden box to show the special ambience of the hotel. Materials used included Cartão Cinza paper for the cover and 120gsm Rives Tradition Pale Cream paper for the text pages.

Burstbound

In this method of binding, sections of the book are glued rather than sewn in. While stronger than perfect binding, the resultant bind is not as strong as that achieved with thread-sewn sections.

#099
Tim Richardson

+**Design Firm** Wishart Design
+**Website** www.wishartdesign.com
+**Client** Tim Richardson

+**Creative Director** Zoë Wishart
+**Designer** Zoë Wishart
+**Printer/Production** Peachy Print, Definitive group, Spitting Image

Wishart Design created this promotional book to raise the international profile of photographer Tim Richardson. It worked closely with Richardson and its book layout showcased his project—<u>Doppelganger</u>. The book was printed in CMYK on 140gsm Splendorgel.

One image from the project was selected, manipulated, and developed into an A1 (594 × 841mm/23½ × 33in) spot-varnished UV screen-printed poster. This was then wrapped around the book and hand-stitched onto the spine.

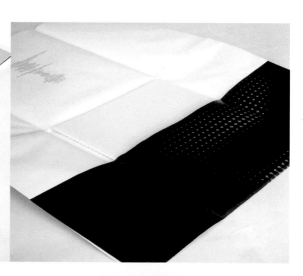

#100
The Brand Distillery

+**Design Firm** Aloof Design
+**Website** www.aloofdesign.com
+**Client** The Brand Distillery

+**Creative Director** Sam Aloof
+**Designer** Andrew Scrase
+**Printer/Production** Aurora

Aloof's hand-laced invitation for the launch of the U'Luvka Vodka Magnum was a direct response to the core values of the brand: simplicity, sex, femininity, luxury, beauty, style, and the Polish heritage of the vodka's recipe.

Referencing 16th- and 17th-century Polish manuscripts and glassware in its hand-drawn illustrations, Aloof achieved a unity across all elements of the U'Luvka campaign. Print techniques were pushed into new territories by full-bleed gloss foil blocking the front of the invite, with a white foil double-hit on the reverse. The Gruppo Papermill stock was also die-cut, punched, perforated, folded, and strung by hand.

Hand finishing
As there is no machine capable of intricate threading like this, all the invites were individually hand assembled and tied. While labor-intensive and time-consuming, this gives each invite a unique feel.

#101
Tin Tab

+**Design Firm** Aloof Design
+**Website** www.aloofdesign.com
+**Client** Tin Tab

+**Creative Director** Sam Aloof
+**Designers** Jon Hodkinson, Andrew Scrase
+**Printer/Production** Longridge

Tin Tab is a Sussex-based manufacturer of interior furniture, buildings, and staircases. To help promote its staircase service at London's 100% Detail Exhibition, it commissioned Aloof to create a 3-D mailer that could be handed out in person or mailed as a follow-up tool.

The mailer was printed CMYK both sides on 300gsm Zen from GF Smith. Finishing included die-cutting, perforation, creasing, and hand-folding.

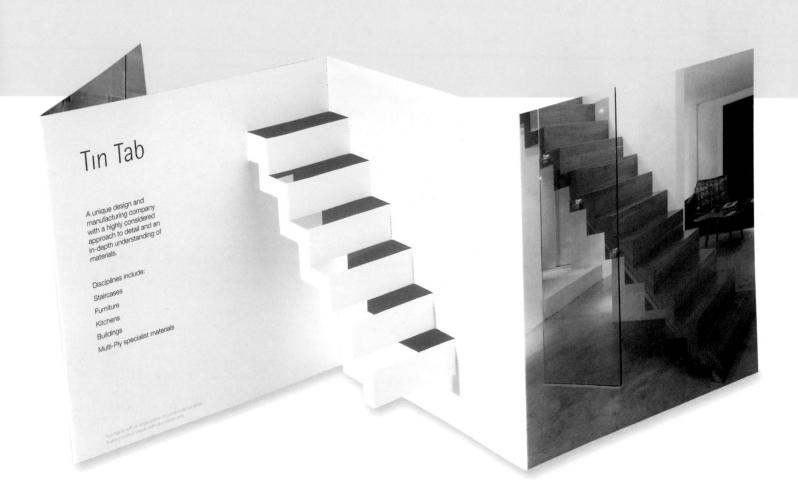

Slide binding

For this piece of promotional literature, the BBC's Creative Services chose to avoid using staples, glue, or any form of conventional binding. Instead, they cut opposing half-length slots on the folds of each double-page spread and hand fed all the spreads into each other, thus locking them together.

#102
BBC

+**Design Firm** Creative Services (BBC)
+**Client** BBC Worldwide

+**Creative Director** Simon Blackwell
+**Designer** Simon Blackwell
+**Printer/Production** Ingersol

Simon Blackwell's promotional material for Tightrope Pictures' BBC production of <u>Dad</u> used a clean format to reflect the issue of "elder abuse." Printed on 300gsm Challenger, the piece was finished with latex, giving the absorbent uncoated stock an unusual finish. Rather than stitching, two slits provided an alternative binding solution.

#103
AIGA

+**Design Firm** Design Army
+**Website** www.designarmy.com
+**Client** American Institute of Graphic Arts

+**Creative Directors** Pum Lefebure, Jake Lefebure
+**Designer** Dan Alder
+**Printer/Production** Colourcraft of Virginia

This invitation by Design Army for the American Institute of Graphic Arts' (AIGA) annual 50 Books/50 Covers awards looks to the little things in life that unexpectedly inspire. It was printed CMYK plus a single spot color and spot varnish on an A1 (594 × 841mm/23½ × 33in) sheet of 80gsm Mohawk Superfine. The intricate die-cut invitation folds down in a clockwise fashion to an undersize A4 (210 × 297mm/8¼ × 11¾in) booklet.

#104
Composite Projects

+**Design Firm** Composite Projects
+**Website** www.composite-projects.com
+**Client** Composite Projects

+**Creative Directors** Mark Gwiazda,
 Christine Fent
+**Designer** Composite Projects
+**Printer/Production** Principal Colour

Composite Projects created this promotional piece targeted at green business to showcase its belief that environmentally friendly production doesn't need to compromise the design. The brochure eliminates wasteful packaging by enveloping its own contents, the outer cover being robust enough to withstand the postal system. Two concealed magnetic strips hold it all together and alleviate the need for stickers. It was only printed in two colors, but through overprinting on two different-colored recycled paper stocks, it incorporated a palette of six colors.

The cover used one spot color on Fenner Paper's 270gsm Colorset Lemon. The inside of the brochure was printed in two spot colors on 120gsm Lemon and 120gsm Ash.

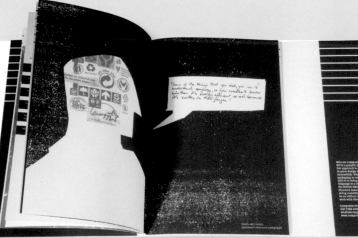

Magnetic binding

Composite Projects wanted this brochure to be self-closing without the aid of stickers. To achieve this, they hid magnetic strips within the folds of the front and back covers.

#105
Fredrik Brodén

+**Design Firm** TBA+D
+**Web** www.tbad.ca
+**Client** Fredrik Brodén

+**Creative Director** Tom Brown
+**Designers** Tom Brown, Fredrik Brodén
+**Printer/Production** Benwell-Atkins

TBA+D's mailer for Frederik Brodén gave the company several production concerns regarding how it would align when closed and how it would lie when placed flat. TBA+D knew it wanted the cover to have a plastic and high-production look, but without resorting to an overly heavy stock. The magnetic strips used to seal the cover when closed posed the problem of unintentional misalignment, which would cause the cover to bend and look awkward if they worked with a cover stock that was too flexible. With both these potential problems in mind, TBA+D really leaned on the experience of their print and production coordinator Ian Roote. His experimentation with various stocks and laminates, and hand-folded and scored models, was crucial in resolving all of these issues. The mailer used six colors with flood gloss varnish, laminates, 5mm Delustered Poly 1, Utopia Premium Gloss for the cover, and various spot matte varnishes.

Double inserts
Two separate concertina booklets have been glued into one cover, allowing for both booklets to open up and fold out at the same time.

#106
EMMI

+**Design Firm** EMMI
+**Website** www.emmi.co.uk
+**Client** EMMI

+**Creative Director** Emmi Salonen
+**Designer** Emmi Salonen
+**Printer/Production** Yellow pages: in-house; other pages: vegetable inks by Print Station

This mailer self-promoting the work of London designer Emmi Salonen can be tailored for specific prospective clients. The mailer consisted of two sections (yellow and white), each of which was bound within a "shell" of 100 percent recycled Colorset Ash using a rubber band.

The yellow section, which was on a Sappi Heritage recycled stock, can be updated by laser printing in a single black. The other full-color section printed on Neptune Unique paper can be reordered depending on the recipient (book for publishers, CD for record companies, etc.).

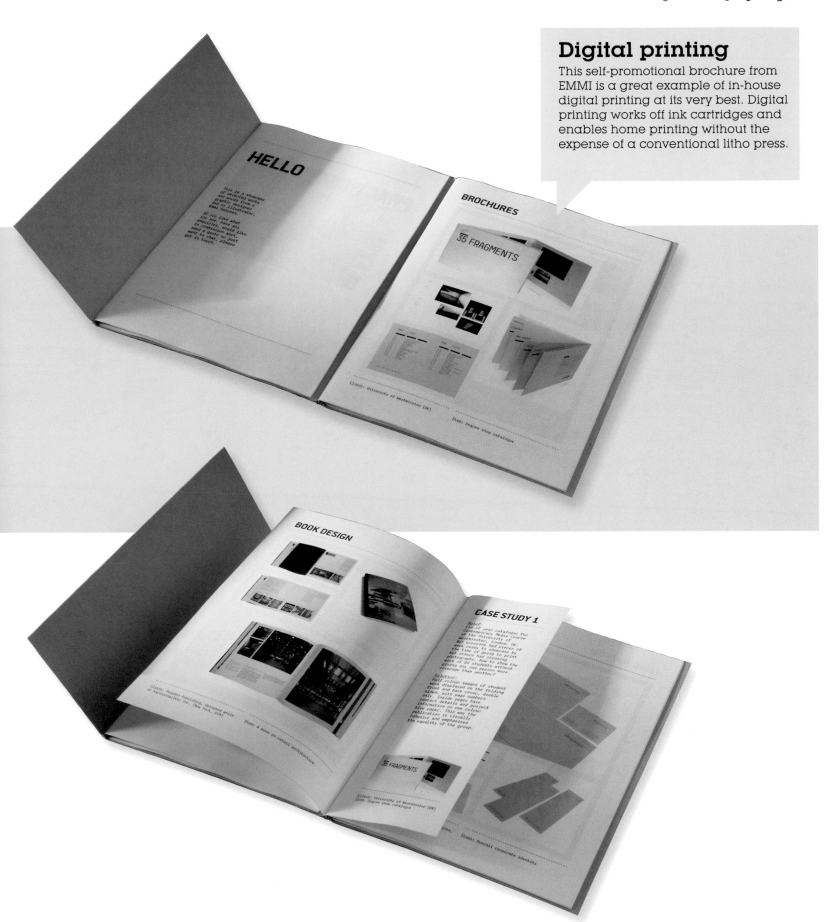

Digital printing

This self-promotional brochure from EMMI is a great example of in-house digital printing at its very best. Digital printing works off ink cartridges and enables home printing without the expense of a conventional litho press.

#107
Dalton Maag

+**Design Firm** Mode
+**Website** www.mode-online.co.uk
+**Client** Dalton Maag

+**Creative Directors** Phil Costin, Ian Styler
+**Designer** Richie Clarke
+**Printer/Production** Good News Press

Mode designed a catalog to celebrate 15 years of Dalton Maag's work in designing custom typefaces and logos for some of the world's leading brands. The front section of the 128-page catalog was printed on lightweight 55gsm TerStar Offset White by Tervakoski. The transparency of the paper echoed the layout pads used to sketch and initiate the ideas of each new font.

In contrast, the back section of the catalog presented a broad selection of completed projects printed on high-gloss Revive stock, with metallic gray ink. The catalog's poster wrap was produced on 90gsm Chromolux 700 and the cover on 260gsm Zeta Smooth White, both from Zanders.

French-folding

French-folding involves a multiple fold in which the paper is folded in half in one direction, folded again perpendicular to the first fold, and bound along the open edges.

#108
Nevis Design Consultants

+**Design Firm** Nevis Design Consultants
+**Website** www.nevisdesign.co.uk
+**Client** Nevis Design Consultants

+**Creative Director** Graham Scott
+**Designer** Stuart Spence
+**Printer/Production** Beith Printing

In this self-promotional piece for Edinburgh-based Nevis Design, the materials were chosen because of their diversity and contrast. Nevis experienced minor problems with the binding—it chose to try several different types of sewing and various treads to get the desired result. Any initial problems were solved through good collaboration with Beith Printing and the binders Hipwells.

Stock and finishing included Bedrock duplexed to Colorplan Cobalt, stab stitched, 3-hole singer-sewn, and foil blocked. Text pages used 50gsm biblio finished with French-folding and the cover used 2,000 micron Bedrock.

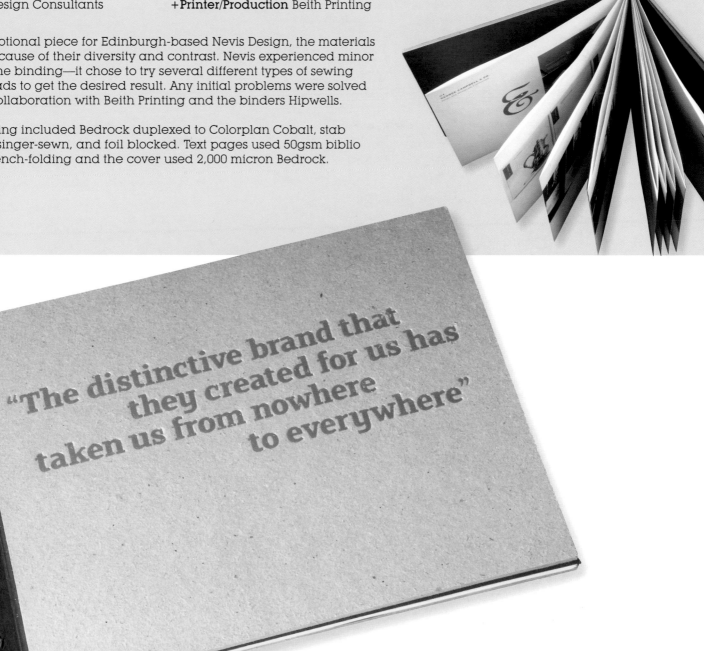

"The distinctive brand that they created for us has taken us from nowhere to everywhere"

#109
OrangeYouGlad

+**Design Firm** OrangeYouGlad
+**Website** www.orangeyouglad.com
+**Client** OrangeYouGlad

+**Creative Director** Tamara Duncan
+**Designers** Tamara Duncan, Erin Shigaki
+**Printer/Production** cover: Little Rhody Press

OrangeYouGlad collected scary stories from friends and family and compiled them into this nifty little Halloween promotional book. The Little Bleak Book served as OrangeYouGlad's annual "thank you" to clients, contributors, vendors, consultants, and other associates. The 44-page book was printed on Strathmore Writing paper at a copy shop. The Carnival Vellum cover was white foil stamped and trimmed by Little Rhody Press. OrangeYouGlad used a Japanese binding technique to bind the books in-house.

Japanese binding

Holes were punched through the book near the spine and the pages stitched together. Any thread can be used, from carpet thread to nylon thread, and even waxed dental floss. A length eight times the book's height is required.

#110
Percept Creative Group

+**Design Firm** Percept Creative Group
+**Website** www.percept.com.au
+**Client** Percept Creative Group

+**Creative Director** Lewis Jenkins
+**Designer** Lewis Jenkins
+**Printer/Production** Jarvis Print

This self-promotional mailer by Australian agency Percept engaged the reader by utilizing interesting production techniques including die-cut and extra foldout pages to impress the reader and make the experience a more memorable one. Stock included 120gsm and 225gsm Knight White Smooth. The text pages were finished by hand with diagonal folding.

Die-cutting

Percept Creative have used die-cutting very cleverly here to make it appear as though the business card is actually held in place by the fingers.

have kept your attention so far,
gine what we could do for your company!

PERCEPT CREATIVE GROUP

Lewis Jenkins
Principal
Creative Director

PO Box 189	T	F	M	lewis@	www.
(4/70 Croydon St)	02	02	0411	percept.	percept.
Cronulla	9544	9544	586	com.au	com.au
NSW 2230	3200	5600	000		

#111
Concordia University

+**Design Firm** ±
+**Website** www.plusminus.ca
+**Client** Concordia University

+**Creative Directors** Peter Crnokrak,
 Michael Longford
+**Designer** Peter Crnokrak
+**Printer/Production** InterContinental Printers

Concordia University's Design Art program emphasizes a multidisciplinary approach to design that also emphasizes the connection between hand and computer work.

Canadian designers ± graphically represented this with 2,000 hand-constructed graduate certificate brochures. A lengthy production process involved metallic spray-paint stencils, three-color offset Pantone printing (black, metallic silver, and opaque white) on Speckletone Kraft paper, and hand-finishing. The final piece achieved an effect more akin to foil blocking, and the use of opaque white created subtle highlight effects.

Stenciling

Creating a stencil or mask allows for hand-finishing the same pattern time and time again. Created using spray paint, stenciling really adds to the depth and quality of this flyer for Concordia University.

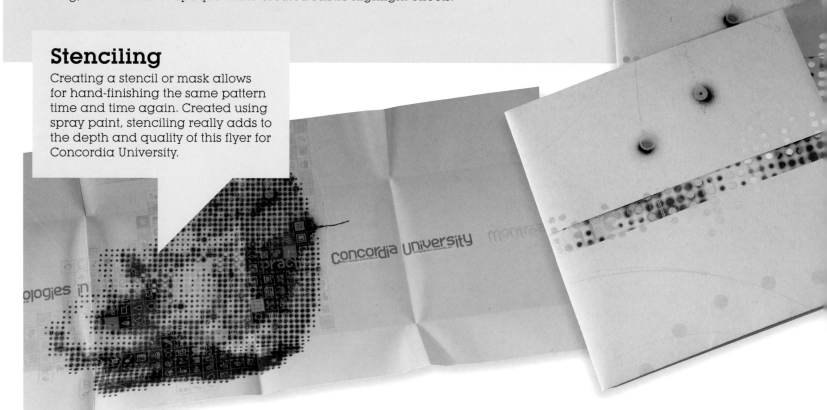

#112
Land Securities

+**Design Firm** Radford Wallis
+**Web** www.radfordwallis.com
+**Client** Land Securities

+**Creative Directors** Stuart Radford, Andrew Wallis
+**Designer** Phil Bold
+**Printer/Production** Boss Print

Property developer Land Securities produce quarterly newsletters to help keep the local community in touch with what is happening on their sites. The brief to Radford Wallis was to create a generic format that could be used for all their various developments. These newsletters were to be delivered direct to local residents, so they needed to be sealed in a self-containing way. The solution was to create a concertina that incorporated the masthead, held the reply card in place, and folded together to seal itself. Radford Wallis opted to use James McNaughton's Incarda Silk 240gsm with die-cut finishing.

Hand-fed loose-leaf

Loose-leaf inserts were ingeniously held in place by die-cutting a tab from the back to marry up with die-cut slits throughout this concertina-folded document. Loose-leaf pages can be added as the tab punches through all the pages and out onto the front cover, holding everything together.

Finishing and Sealing

AIGA 50 CALL FOR INSPIRATIONS

Laser cutting

This is possibly one of the best examples of just how precise and detailed laser-cutting results can be. This level of detail simply couldn't be achieved with conventional die-cutting.

#113
Jason Bruges Studio

+**Design Firm** BB/Saunders
+**Website** www.bbsaunders.com
+**Client** Jason Bruges Studio

+**Creative Director** Warren Beeby
+**Designer** Phil Evans
+**Printer/Production** Trilogy Lasercraft, Identity Print

Jason Bruges Studio produces work including interactive light sculptures, interactive environments, events, and screen-based installations. It explores the use of interactivity with the public and the environment through the use of imaginative technologies. BB/Saunders created an identity that utilized light and allowed interactivity. The logo, based on a variation of a popular configuration of dot matrix LED lights, was laser cut through each stationery item allowing light to pass through. In addition to the laser-cut logo, the folder and letterhead have a grid of perforated disks which, when pressed out, let the user personalize each item with words, numbers, or symbols.

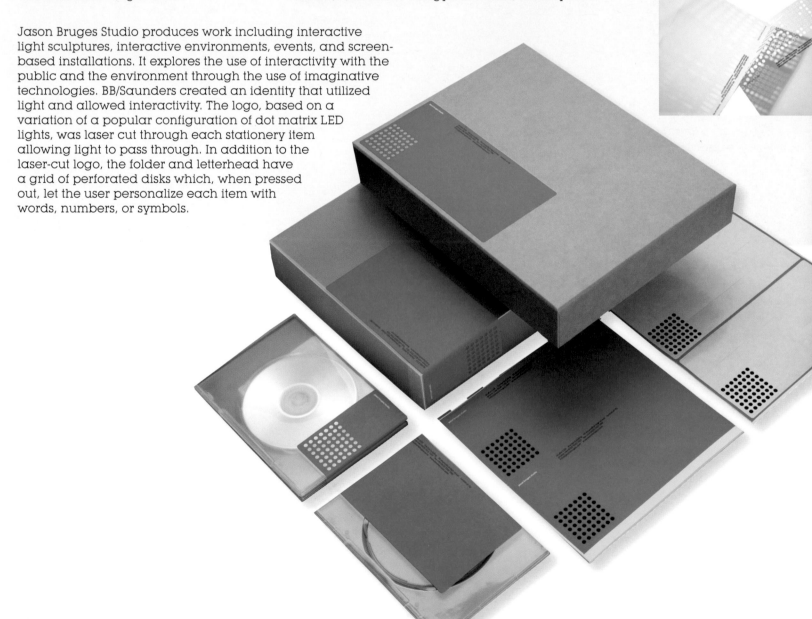

jason bruges studio

#114
AIGA

+**Design Firm** Design Army
+**Website** www.designarmy.com
+**Client** American Institute of Graphic Arts

+**Creative Directors** Pum Lefebure, Jake Lefebure
+**Designer** Dan Alder
+**Printer/Production** Colourcraft of Virginia

Design Army's second part of the invitation to the American Institute of Graphic Arts' (AIGA) annual 50 Books/50 Covers awards creates a visually stunning pack that contains all the relevant literature as well as massive foldout posters. Printed by Colourcraft using CMYK plus a single spot colour and spot varnish onto an A1 (594 × 841mm/23½ × 33in) sheet of 80gsm Mohawk Superfine. (See also page 147.)

Cross-folding

Design Army wanted to produce a large-format, A1 (594 × 841mm/23½ × 33in) poster, but this had to fit within an A4 (210 × 297mm/8⅛ × 11⅝in) pack. By cross-folding, using multiple counter folds, the A1 poster folds down easily to the required size.

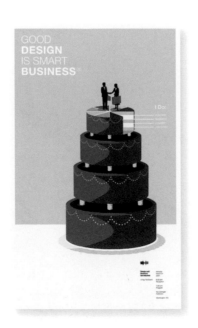

115
Gavin Martin Associates

+**Design Firm** NB: Studio
+**Website** www.nbstudio.co.uk
+**Client** Gavin Martin Associates

+**Creative Directors** Alan Dye, Nick Finney, Ben Stott
+**Designer** Daniel Lock
+**Printer/Production** Gavin Martin, NB: Studio

Printer Gavin Martin Associates asked NB: Studio to design a direct mailer to announce its move to new offices in the Tea Building in Shoreditch, London. Inspired by its new location, NB:Studio decided lavishly to letterpress the typography on GF Smith card and then painstakingly hand stain all 1,000 cards with a tea ring to reflect the idea of removal and removal men leaving tea stains all over the office.

The A6 (105 × 148mm/4 × 5¾in) finished mailer was printed black and Cool Grey 8 on 320gsm Accent Antique Archival by GF Smith. The tea stains were printed by hand with real tea substituting CMYK with Earl Grey, Darjeeling, Rooibos, and English Breakfast teas.

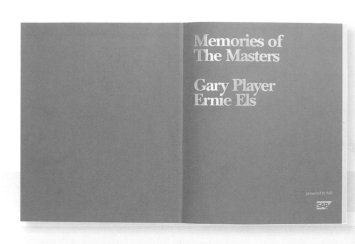

#116
SAP

+**Design Firm** Sixfive Design
+**Web** www.sixfive.com
+**Clients** SAP, The Works London

+**Creative Director** Al Kennedy
+**Designer** Sixfive Design
+**Printer/Production** Various

Guests of SAP at The Masters 2005 golf tournament were presented with a beautifully crafted, handbound book written by Ernie Els and Gary Player, giving their personal views of the tournament, along with an itinerary for the weekend. Cover material was Matrix Embossed White from GF Smith, with text foil blocking on the front and back covers. The text pages were litho printed onto 135gsm PhoeniXmotion, with eight pages screen printed white onto 135gsm Emerald Colorplan, also from GF Smith, with silver foil–blocked endpapers.

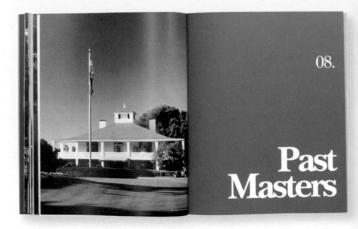

Channel binding

Channel binding can be carried out on both paperback and hardback publications. It provides a relatively cheap, but highly professional-looking binding for anything from book publications to conference notes and brochures.

#117
Oslo Cuatro

+**Design Firm** Serial Cut
+**Website** www.serialcut.com
+**Client** Oslo Cuatro

+**Creative Director** Sergio del Puerto
+**Designer** Sergio del Puerto
+**Printer/Production** TF Artes Gráficas

747 Lounge Bar is an elegant, futuristic bar for stewards and pilots, close to Madrid's airport. Serial Cut™ needed to create the same elegance in this promotional piece. This was achieved by foil stamping the silver logotype on 160gsm Plastic Mellow paper with silver reflection, and printing one Pantone metallic ink.

#118
The Hospital

+**Design Firm** Spin
+**Website** www.spin.co.uk
+**Client** The Hospital

+**Creative Director** Tony Brook
+**Designer** Spin
+**Printer/Production** Tradewinds

The promotional mailer for private members' club The Hospital focused on its opulent interiors. Images of the club's environment of richly patterned wallpapers and upholstery were printed on 215gsm Splendorlux paper in an eight-panel concertina piece. On the reverse, uncoated side, the same images were overprinted with black to create a subtle echo of the original images as well as a surface for the text, which was silk screen printed in silver. The Hospital's "H" marque was ram punched through the folded mailer, giving glimpses of the full-color image of a panel of decorative wallpaper. It was all held together with a branded sticker ready for mailing.

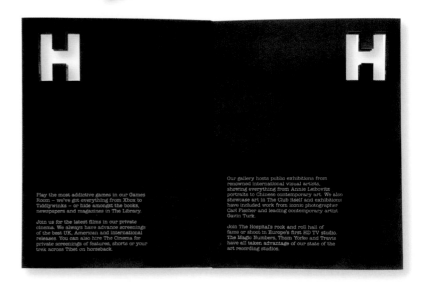

Ram punching

This technique allows for the precise, accurate, and deep punching and cutting of shapes from card/paper where there is a larger depth or quantity than conventional die-cutting can manage. Ram punching can cut through hundreds of pages in seconds.

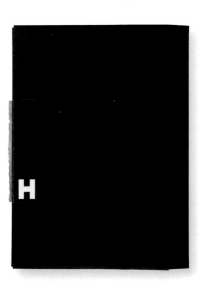

#119
Acorn Conceptual Textiles

+**Design Firm** Studio Output
+**Website** www.studio-output.com
+**Client** Acorn Conceptual Textiles

+**Creative Director** Steve Payne
+**Designer** Steve Payne
+**Printer/Production** Plan 4 Print

Studio Output's identity for Acorn, a conceptual textiles house that creates swatches for high-end fashion labels, was based on its interpretation of the word "acorn." Utilizing drawn tree elements, the logo was combined with varying textured and patterned backdrops to create a juxtaposition of form and tone. These elements were changed seasonally in Acorn's catalogs to represent the changes in color, texture, and materials used in the collection. Die-cuts and UV laminates on the business cards and presentation folders further enhanced the decorative and tactile qualities of the designs.

ROMANTIQUE
A transitional large scale floral and leaf tapestry

#120
Third Eye Design

+**Design Firm** Third Eye Design
+**Website** www.thirdeyedesign.co.uk
+**Client** Third Eye Design

+**Creative Director** Kenny Allan
+**Designer** Kenny Allan
+**Printer/Production** Beith Printing

US promotes the work of Glasgow/New York agency Third Eye Design. Featuring nine case studies that emphasize "design effectiveness," the work in the book is visible across a vast range of industries from finance to fashion and from architecture to the arts.

The cover was made of fabric stretched over board, which was debossed with the title letters "US."

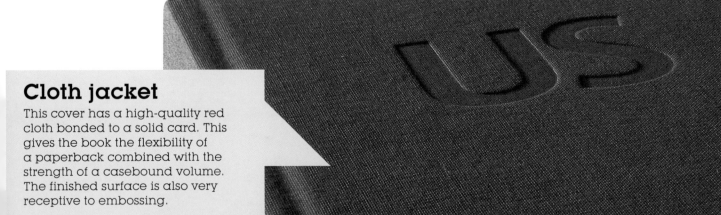

Cloth jacket

This cover has a high-quality red cloth bonded to a solid card. This gives the book the flexibility of a paperback combined with the strength of a casebound volume. The finished surface is also very receptive to embossing.

#121
Anti-Slavery International

+**Design Firm** Inaria
+**Website** www.inaria-design.com
+**Client** Anti-Slavery International

+**Creative Directors** Andrew Thomas, Debora Berardi
+**Designers** Anna Leaver, Anup Sharma-Yun
+**Printer/Production** Fulmar

Anti-Slavery is a charity working exclusively against slavery and related abuses. Its annual fund-raising ball is an essential part of its income. Each year its chosen theme ensures the seriousness of the message is well delivered. The theme "Colors of the World" inspired Inaria to produce a program that was relevant to the slave trade, while allowing a positive and relevant message by using color. Six different-colored posters, designed to decorate the walls of the event, also folded down to become dust jackets for the program itself. Distinctly colored sections within the brochure, stenciled die-cut typography on each of the divider pages, and brightly colored paper stocks were all used in tandem with real-life imagery to create a strong graphic language.

Flush trimming
The uncoated pulp-board cover has been drilled and screw-bound to the text pages. The cover boards have been flush trimmed to the exact width of these text pages to give the book a solid and precise hard edge.

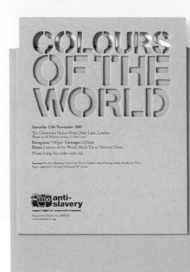

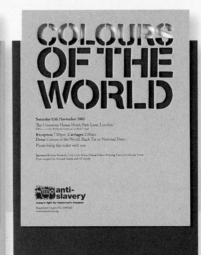

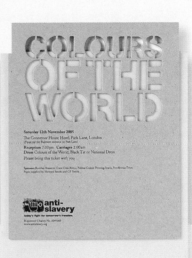

In-line sealer

Used heavily throughout this booklet, sealer varnishes are often printed in-line as a fifth plate. The varnish seals the color to the paper to avoid rub off, especially where there are large areas of blank white space opposite areas of laid-down print.

#122
VH1

+**Design Firm** dixonbaxi
+**Web** www.dixonbaxi.com
+**Client** VH1

+**Creative Directors** Simon Dixon, Aporva Baxi
+**Designer** dixonbaxi
+**Printer/Production** G&B Printers

This limited-edition book by dixonbaxi for music video channel VH1 was designed to reflect the shape of the VH1 logo when opened. dixonbaxi opted to shun the rules when designing the brand's style guidelines manual in favor of a creative exploration of what VH1 stands for. Only 250 copies of the gilt-edged book were made.

#123
TheatreWorks

+**Design Firm** fFurious
+**Website** www.ffurious.com
+**Client** TheatreWorks

+**Creative Director** Little Ong
+**Designer** Joanne Tay
+**Printer/Production** Fabulous Printers Pte Ltd.

A converted rice warehouse, 72–13 is the new home of
TheatreWorks. The space can be a gallery, cinema, or theatre,
though its primary purpose is to support local and international
creativity and expression. With the transitory nature of the space,
creatives and viewers could enter it with one frame of mind and
leave with another. To symbolize this idea, the travelator was
selected as a graphic icon to be used across various materials.
The materials suggest the openness of the space through their
minimalist look. The invitation card was kept clean with a
one-color metallic print on 240gsm white card. The travelator
graphic icon was then embossed across the invitation, giving
the design a sense of open space.

#124
Land Securities

+**Design Firm** Hat-Trick Design
+**Website** www.hat-trickdesign.co.uk
+**Client** Land Securities

+**Creative Directors** David Kimpton, Jim Sutherland, Gareth Howat
+**Designers** David Kimpton, Jim Sutherland, Gareth Howat
+**Printer/Production** Boss Print

Advertising space was about to become available to rent at one of London's top tourist spots, Piccadilly Circus. The owners of the "Piccadilly Lights" site, Land Securities approached Hat-Trick to produce a brochure that presented not only the important technical information, but also the heritage of the site.

The brochure featured a foil-finished cover on Baladek Fluctuations with singer-sewn binding. The text pages were printed on 200gsm Hannoart Silk with additional acetate pages on clear PVK 130mm. The brochure sits inside an acetate sleeve.

Singer-sewn

Singer-sewn binding is ideal for short-run publications with a fair quantity of pages. It is particularly good for single-section books, which can then be inserted into case covers.

#125
Barnickel, Houston

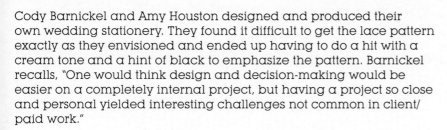

+**Design Firm** Barnickel
+**Website** www.barnickel.us
+**Clients** Barnickel, Houston

+**Creative Director** Cody Barnickel
+**Designers** Cody Barnickel, Amy Houston
+**Printer/Production** Matador Press

Cody Barnickel and Amy Houston designed and produced their own wedding stationery. They found it difficult to get the lace pattern exactly as they envisioned and ended up having to do a hit with a cream tone and a hint of black to emphasize the pattern. Barnickel recalls, "One would think design and decision-making would be easier on a completely internal project, but having a project so close and personal yielded interesting challenges not common in client/paid work."

Materials used included museum board, eyelets, ribbon, wastenot paper envelopes, string, magnets, weatherproof labels, bottles, and aluminum caps, all printed using traditional letterpressing.

#126
Keep Left Studio

+**Design Firm** Keep Left Studio
+**Website** www.keepleftstudio.com
+**Client** Keep Left Studio

+**Creative Director** Kevin Yo
+**Designer** Keep Left Studio
+**Printer/Production** Precision 20/20

Limited to 1,000 hand-numbered copies, Kleft is the 100-page magazine from
Keep Left Studio in Sydney, Australia. Each magazine has its own special laser-cut
protective 330gsm card sleeve. Kleft covers many art-related issues, including
what inspires some of the images people produce and what drives creatives to do
what they do in compiling a human image bank. Its goal is to produce something
meaningful for everyone within its pages.

Kleft uses laser-cut card sleeves on 330gsm Matt Sovereign Silk stock with
hand-folded and taped finishing.

Pin perforation

Pin perforation uses a special die plate to create a precise perforation that allows the paper to be torn cleanly by hand. The most common form of pin perforation can be clearly seen on modern postage stamps.

#127
3

+**Design Firm** 3
+**Website** www.whois3.com
+**Client** 3

+**Creative Director** Sam Maclay
+**Designer** Tim McGrath
+**Printer/Production** Crack Press

In its self-promotional ID package, US agency 3 wanted to reinforce its name by doing "3 things" about each employee and itself. Putting the package together involved a lot of work for 3. Most agencies would not be willing to put the handwork into something like this, considering it to be impractical on a large scale. 3 managed to keep it fun by producing the package in small batches. For 3, the labor involved was outweighed by the chance to do something different.

Materials used included French Paper's Frostone Arctic for the letterhead and business cards, with French Dur-o-tune Butcher Orange for the envelopes. Labels were offset printed, pin perfed, and then applied. The letterhead package was letterpressed, pin perfed, and hand-assembled.

#128
EMI Records

+**Design Firm** Wallzo
+**Web** www.wallzo.com
+**Client** EMI Records

+**Creative Director** Darren Wall
+**Designer** Darren Wall
+**Printer/Production** EMI Records

For Hot Chip's first EMI release, The Warning, Wallzo developed a metaphor for the Hot Chip sound—colorful toy blocks with plastic wedges forced into them represent the awkward, but appealing way different sounds are combined on the album. Wallzo decided to print on the reverse of the board with a machine seal to give it a tactile, handcrafted feel. Granted a little more freedom with the 12" edition, and briefed to design a truly desirable piece, Wallzo used a debossing pattern to create a collectible object—something tactile and crafted.

Scoring

With stock that is heavier than 200gsm, it is advisable to score the paper or card (creating a groove) prior to folding. Scoring facilitates bending, and so avoids cracking or damaging the material itself.

Glossary

Bleed

Engraving

Letterpress

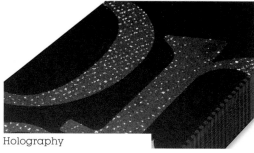
Holography

Halftone

Duotone

Printing

Bit-map
A generic style of computer-originated typeface, constructed pixel by pixel. The term is also used to describe the pixelation of a digital image.

Bleed
The term used to refer to an element printed beyond the trimmed edge of the page, allowing the image, rule, or type to extend to the very edge of the printed page.

CMYK
Stands for cyan, magenta, yellow, and key (black). These primary ink colors are combined on a press to produce a full range of color. Also known as full- or 4-color printing.

Digital printing
Digital printing is the reproduction of digital images on a physical surface, such as common or photographic paper, film, cloth, plastic, etc.

Duotone
A halftone made of two colors, i.e., where two colors are printed together to make an image richer and denser in color.

Engraving/etched plates
Printing method using a metal plate with an image cut or acid etched into its surface.

Halftone
A process used to reproduce an illustration, which involves breaking it up into small dots of different densities to simulate a full tonal range.

Holography
Using lasers to overlay embossed images onto film, then paper to produce the appearance of a 3-D image.

Inks (specials, metallics, fluorescents)
Most mass-produced books are printed using lithographic inks. As a rule, full-color printing is achieved through the combination of the four process colors: cyan, magenta, yellow, and black. However, additional "special" inks (such as fluorescents or metallics) can also be used to produce distinctive results.

Letterpress
A traditional method of printing type, using a series of metal stamps with individual letters cast into the surface. The printed sheet becomes more tactile than that produced by conventional offset lithographic printing, because the type becomes debossed into the surface.

Offset-lithography
The standard format of printing where an image on a plate is "offset" to a rubber blanket cylinder which, in turn, transfers the image to a sheet of paper.

Raster imaging
An alternative method of halftone screening using an electron beam. It creates complex, irregular patterns of very fine dots and produces higher-quality images and color work.

Reversed type
Letters are left unprinted, with the surrounding area printed, to allow the type to reveal the color of the stock.

Spot color

Concertina fold

Scoring

Woodblock/rubber die

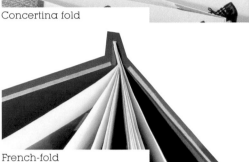

French-fold

Throw-outs

Silk screen

Cross-fold

Roll-fold

RGB
Red, green, blue: the three primary colors used onscreen to generate a full spectrum of color.

Silk screen
The method of printing by which ink is forced through a stencil glued to a mesh or screen. Also referred to as screen printing or serigraphy.

Spot color
A special color not generated by the 4-color process method, often from the PANTONE swatch range.

Vignette
A graduated tint by which one color fades into another color or white.

Woodblock/rubber die
Letters carved in pieces of wood or rubber to be relief-printed; similar to letterpress.

Folding

Concertina fold
Pages folded in a zigzag manner, like the bellows of a concertina. The paper can be extended to its full length with a single pull. Also known as fan folding or accordian folding.

Cross-fold
Where a printed page is folded, then turned over and folded in the opposite direction to give multiple folds similar to those of a map.

French-fold
The method of folding a page in half and binding along the open edges.

Gatefold
Folding where the outer edges fold inward to meet the gutter, creating an 8-page effect. Often used on center-page spreads to create impact.

Perforated fold
Printing sheets are perforated prior to folding the sheets down to the page size. This allows French-folded pages to be torn open easily.

Roll-fold
A process whereby a long sheet of paper is folded into panels or pages starting from the far right, with each subsequent panel folded back toward the left—effectively it is rolled back around itself.

Scoring
Required on heavier paper (200gsm and above) to allow folding to work properly. On thicker card scoring is required, otherwise the edges can crack badly.

Throw-outs
Where the page size of a document is bigger than its finished size, but folded in on itself to fit within the document. This allows for bigger pages than those of standard sizes.

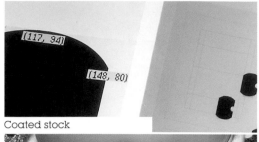
Coated stock

Perspex

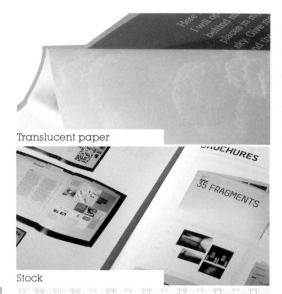
Translucent paper

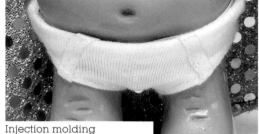
Injection molding

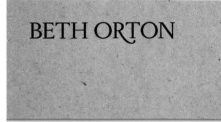
Pulp board

Stock

Cast-coated

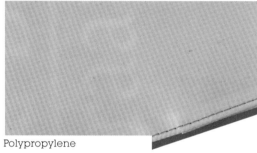
Polypropylene

Uncoated stock

Materials

Cast-coated
Paper that has a very high-quality, high-gloss surface on one side, while the reverse remains matte and uncoated. Achieved by pressing the paper against a metal drum while the clay coating is still wet.

Coated stock
A smooth, hard-surfaced paper good for reproducing halftone images. It is created by coating the surface with china clay.

Cover/bookbinding board
A dense, coated fiberboard used for the covers of casebound books.

Injection molding
This process is used to produce large quantities of identical plastic items. It uses high-impact polystyrenes (HIPS).

Kraft paper
Strong paper made from unbleached wood pulp. This material is often used for paper bags and wrapping paper due to its strength.

Perspex
Perspex is a trade name in many countries in Europe for polymethyl methacrylate. It is tough plastic, first produced in 1930 and widely used for advertising signs and protective shields. It is manufactured under other names: Plexiglas, Lucite, Acrylite, and Rhoplex.

Polypropylene
A flexible plastic sheet available in many different colors, including clear and frosted.

Pulp board
Pulp board is very thick with a rough recycled feel. A highly absorbent, flexible and resilient sheet which allows ink to soak into it, giving it a very rustic feel.

Ream
Five hundred sheets of any type of paper.

Signature
A printed sheet folded at least once to become part of a printed piece. Signatures are usually made up in sets of four, eight, sixteen, etc.

Simulator paper
A thin, translucent paper, more commonly known as tracing paper.

Stock
The paper or other material on which a job is printed.

Translucent paper
Translucent paper is an almost see-through/transparent stock that allows some light through it in an attractive way, making it perfect for overlays.

Uncoated stock
Paper that has a rougher surface than coated paper and is not coated with clay. Because of this it is both bulkier and more opaque.

Binding tape

Perfect binding

Casebound

Burstbound

Saddle-stitching

Japanese binding

Magnetic binding

Singer-sewn binding

Post/screw binding

Binding

Binding tape
Tape or other material that binds around the spine of a book to protect the edges and allow for easy opening.

Burstbound
The pages of the document are gathered, but not sewn with thread. The folded edges are perforated and glue is inserted, which soaks into the perfs.

Casebound
Binding using glue to hold sections of pages (signatures) to a case made of thick board bound in plastic, fabric, or leather.

Channel binding
A mechanical binding system that uses a metal U-channel built into a one-piece cover. No punching or gluing is required, and a number of systems allow for a limited de-binding of documents.

Japanese binding
Thread is bound from the back to the front of the book around the outside edge of the spine. Used primarily for binding loose sheets.

Magnetic binding
Used only on outer covers; magnets are attached to added folds, allowing the outer cover to snap shut.

Perfect binding
Pages are glued to the cover and held together with a strip of adhesive, giving the spine of the brochure a completely flat appearance.

Post/screw binding
Pages are secured using bolts inserted through drilled holes and secured on the reverse with a post.

Saddle-stitching
The standard method of binding for literature; pages are secured with stitches or staples placed through the centerfold of nested signatures.

Side stitching
Pages are stapled and bound together along one edge. Also known as sidewire.

Singer-sewn binding
Sewing along the centerfold of a document using an industrial version of the household sewing machine.

Wire/comb binding
The teeth of a plastic comb or thin metal wire are inserted through holes on a stack of paper, locking the pages into the binding mechanism.

Forme cut

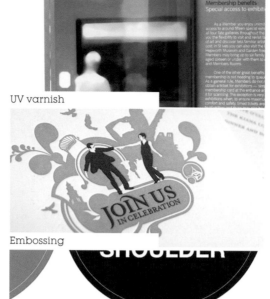
UV varnish

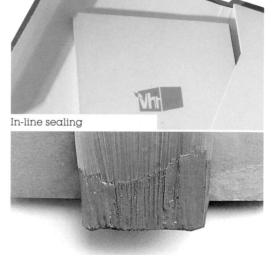
In-line sealing

Foil blocking

Embossing

Hand finishing

Laser die-cut

Kiss cut

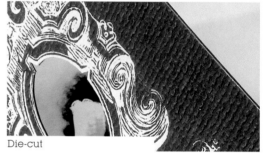
Die-cut

Finishing

Debossing
A surface pattern is pressed into paper or material to leave a recessed impression; also known as blind embossing.

Die-cut
Where a decorative or unusual cut is created within the inside of a document or page. It is created using a die which comprises sharp metal rules mounted on a board or roller and used for stamping.

Embossing
As debossing, but produces a raised impression instead of a recessed one.

Engraving
Printing method using a metal plate with an image cut into its surface that holds ink and is then pressed into the paper.

Foil blocking
A foil and a heated die are brought together and stamped onto paper to form a printed impression.

Forme cut
A die forme is used to cut a document to a non-standard shape.

Gloss/metallic foil
Uses the same process as foil blocking, but a metallic foil is used instead with a gloss printed directly on top.

Hand finishing
Anything that cannot be produced by in-line machinery will require hand finishing. This could be anything from folding in scored pages and throw-outs to inserting added elements or binding a document together by hand.

In-line sealing
During the printing process, instead of an extra color, a thin varnish is printed over large areas of printed material, in effect sealing the page to avoid the ink rubbing off onto opposite pages. Often applied as a fifth color during the CMYK printing process.

Kiss cut
Similar to die-cutting, but does not pass right the way through the sheet. Mostly used for making sticker sheets where the backing paper must remain intact.

Lamination
The application of a protective plastic film over a printed surface or sheet.

Laser die-cut
A very precise method of cutting, this can cope with far more intricate shapes than conventional die-cutting.

Laser etching
Using this process, patterns or text can be written in high resolution and transferred to the underlying material via reactive ion etching.

Pin perforations
Small holes made by puncturing the surface of paper with pins. Mostly used for cutting long series of holes so that paper can be torn more easily.

Ram punch
A ram punch, or punch press, is a machine tool used for cutting precise shapes in metal, card, or paper. It is generally used for heavier cards, or large quantities of paper/card.

UV varnish
A liquid varnish applied and then heat cured with ultraviolet light, resulting in a tough, durable glossy finish.

- **Adelaide, Australia** // Voice
- **Melbourne, Australia** // Famous Visual Services // Standard
- **Sydney, Australia** // Akina // Claretduskymoonpie // Deuce Design // Keep Left Studio // Percept Creative Group // Studio Locaso // Wishart Design

- **Antwerp, Belgium** // Sound in Motion
- **Brussels, Belgium** // Coast Design

- **São Paulo, Brazil** // Superbacana Design

- **Montréal, Canada** // ±
- **Québec, Canada** // Philippe Archontakis
- **Port Moody, Canada** // TBA+D

- **Prague, Czech Republic** // Heyduk Musil Strnad

- **Jakarta, Indonesia** // Jejak

- **Tel-Aviv, Israel** // Jewboy

- **Mexico City, Mexico** // Blok Design
- **Roma, Mexico** // Zoveck Estudio

- **Arnhem, the Netherlands** // Catalogtree
- **The Hague, the Netherlands** // Underware
- **Amsterdam, the Netherlands** // QuA Associates // Main Studio

- **Oslo, Norway** // Bleed

- **Manila, Philippines** // Electrolychee
- **Quezon City, Philippines** // Inksurge

- **Lublin, Poland** // Sensual

- **Singapore** // Kinetic // Neighbor // Ffurious // Yucca Studio

- **Barcelona, Spain** // Astrid Stavro
- **Madrid, Spain** // Design People Studio // Serial Cut

- **Stockholm, Sweden** // Märang

- **Zurich, Switzerland** // Joliat

- **Belfast, UK** // Hurson

- **Bristol, UK** // Sixfive Design
- **Cardiff, UK** // Departures
- **Edinburgh, UK** // Whitespace // Nevis Design Consultants
- **Glasgow, UK** // Stand // Third Eye Design // Traffic DC
- **Leeds, UK** // Studio Monkeys // nothingdiluted studios
- **Lewes, UK** // Aloof Design

- **London, UK** // 20/20 // Airside // Andy Smith // BB/Saunders // Composite Projects // Creative Services (BBC) // Deep // dixonbaxi // EMMI // Form // Four IV // Hat-Trick Design // Heard Creative // I Saw It First // Inaria // Mode // Muller // N/A // NB: Studio // Nick Clark Design // Radford Wallis // Saturday // Sea // Spin // Think Tank Media // Thoughtomatic // Tone // Turnbull Grey // Wallzo // You Are Beautiful // Zip Design
- **Nottingham, UK** // Hello Duudle/Wiggleton Press // Studio Output
- **Newark, UK** // Dowling Design & Art Direction
- **Newcastle, UK** // The Military
- **Stoke, UK** // Iwantdesign

- **New Mexico, USA** // 3
- **New Orleans, USA** // Iamalwayshungry
- **New York, USA** // OrangeYouGlad // The Apartment
- **Portland, USA** // Barnickel
- **San Francisco, USA** // Factor Design
- **Seattle, USA** // Ryan Burlinson // Turnstyle
- **Washington, USA** // Design Army

Agency Index

Index

Acknowledgments

Lindy and Tony and **all** at **RotoVision**
Caroline Roberts and **all** at **Grafik**
Patrick Burgoyne and **all** at **Creative Review**
Paul Scharf, GF Smith Paper
Susan Mitchell, Howard Smith Paper
Jamie Douglas, McNaughton Paper
Alex Higgs, Think Tank Media

Special thanks to:
Chris Smith, **Gordon Beveridge**, and **Stephen Kelman** at **Traffic**
Lorna Kilpatrick-Witham the nagging wife, but quite fast at typing
Simon Punter Photographer
Julie Wilkinson Designer

My sincerest thanks to all the companies who submitted work for
this publication, especially for the fantastic work that, in the end,
we were not able to include. If only I could have had more pages!

Scott Witham, 2007

About the Author

A designer with more than 15 years of agency experience, Scott Witham graduated in 1992 from Duncan of Jordanstone College of Art, Scotland, with an Honors degree in graphic design and typography. Over the years he has worked for some of Scotland's best-known agencies, designing for clients including Sony, Orange, LURPAK, Virgin, and the Royal Bank of Scotland Group.

He founded Traffic Design Consultants, where he now works as Creative Director, in 2002. Witham's first book <u>Festive Graphics: The art and design of self promotion</u> was published by RotoVision in 2002. His second book, <u>Touch This: Graphic design that feels good</u> was published by Rockport in 2005.

scott@traffic-design.co.uk